This book isn't just a theological exploration—it's a guide to transforming your life by embracing the truths of who you are in God.
— **Nate Dewberry**, director | The Redeemed

Lies about your worth, your past, and your identity don't get the final word. God does! This book confronts falsehoods and replaces them with Scripture-rooted truth that redefines how you live, believe, and view yourself in Christ.
— **Nathan Roth,** leader | The Forge Men's Ministry

Beautifully written, this book brings to light how God sees us, values us, and His plans to use us. Perfect for everyone needing help transforming from a fractured self-image into their true identity as defined by God.
—**Dave Grimer**, leader | The Redeemed

In our current world, we're constantly bombarded by voices competing for our attention—marketing executives, entertainment and social media trying to define us and tell us our worth. The information, or more accurately, the revelation contained in this book, has never been more relevant. It addresses profound questions like: Who am I? What defines me? Do I have value? Does God love me? Am I even worthy of that love? Jim tackles these questions with humility and truth, drawing from The Word of God, his and the experiences of others. The book paints a beautiful picture of the holistic lives that God intends for us to have in Him, and gives practical steps to living them out. I believe that lives will be transformed as readers begin to see themselves as God sees them.
—**Eze Okebalama**, leader | The Redeemed

IDENTITY REVEALED

As we navigate through life we are met with an onslaught of obstacles; some are bumps while others are mountainous, some easily forgotten with others cutting us deeply. Jim does a wonderful job of reminding us of what our identity in Christ really means; how as a Christian we have been equipped to live a victorious life. As you read this book you will see Jim unfold many of the identities that Christ has given us to be able to overcome barriers and hurdles that can cause us to stumble in our faith and daily relationships with others. The reader is routinely challenged to self-reflect on questions that can help reveal just what is hindering us from personal growth; followed up with a challenge to take action steps to implement what we have just learned, becoming more purposeful and intentional in our lives. Filled with personal stories and testimonies this is a must-read book.
—**Todd Snitker**, leader | The Forge Men's Ministry

Identity Revealed is more than just a devotional, it's a sacred conversation between brothers in Christ. Reading this book felt like sitting down with my friend Jim himself, someone I deeply respect and consider a true friend and warrior in the faith. Jim has walked through real battles, the kind that leave you in the "land of dry bones", but by the life-giving love of Christ, he's come out anointed and full of purpose. This book is the overflow of that journey. It's not laced with lofty theological jargon or polished religiosity. It's raw, honest, and deeply personal. Jim doesn't preach at you, but rather he walks with you, guiding you through the truth of Scripture with the tenderness of someone who's been there and found hope. Reading *Identity Revealed* is like letting a trusted friend take your hand and point you back to who you really are in Christ. Through his vulnerable storytelling, rich biblical insight, and gentle encouragement, Jim reminds us that our true identity is not in what the world says, but in what Jesus has already declared.
—**Payton Linder**, small group coordinator | The Redeemed

IDENTITY REVEALED

A Journey in Discovering Who You Are in Christ

Jim Miner

| JM |

RebrandednChrist, LLC

Identity Revealed

Copyright © 2025 RebrandnChrist, LLC

First Edition: February 2025

Library of Congress Control Number : 979-8-9927465-0-1

All rights reserved. No part of this book may be used or reproduced, stored in a retrieval system, or transmitted in any form or by any means – electronic, mechanical, photocopy, recording, or any other – except in the case of brief quotations in critical articles or reviews, whatsoever without written permission.

Printed in the United States of America.

Jim Miner @ www.rebrandednchrist.com

All Scripture quotations, unless otherwise indicated, are taken from the Holy Bible, New International Version®, NIV®. Copyright ©1973, 1978, 1984, 2011 by Biblica, Inc.™ Used by permission of Zondervan. All rights reserved worldwide. The "NIV" and "New International Version" are trademarks registered in the United States Patent and Trademark Office by Biblica, Inc.™

Scripture taken from the New King James Version®. Copyright © 1982 by Thomas Nelson. Used by permission. All rights reserved.

Scripture taken from the NEW AMERICAN STANDARD BIBLE®, Copyright © 1960, 1962, 1963, 1968, 1971, 1972, 1973, 1975, 1977, 1995 by The Lockman Foundation. Used by permission.

While the author has made every effort to provide accurate Internet addresses at the time of publication, neither the publisher nor the author assumes any responsibility for errors, or for changes that occur after publication. Further, the publisher does not have any control over and does not assume any responsibility for author or third-party websites or their content.

ISBN – 979-8-9927465-1-8 (eBook)
ISBN – 979-8-9927465-3-2 (Hardback)
ISBN – 979-8-9927465-2-5 (audio)

Book design by Jim Miner
Cover design by Jim and Cristee' Miner

identity
_____

iden·ti·ty

1. the distinguishing character or personality of an individual

reveal | revealed
_____

re·veal

1. to make known through divine inspiration

2. to make (something secret or hidden) publicly or generally known

CONTENTS

Dedication	IX
Acknowledgements	X
Forward	XII
Introduction	XV
1. I am Blessed	1
2. I am Chosen	9
3. I am Complete	21
4. I am Confident	31
5. I am a Conqueror	41
6. I Can Do All Things	51
7. I am Fearless	63
8. I Am Forgiven	75
9. I am God's Child	91
10. I am God's Friend	105
11. I am Made by God	115
12. I am an Overcomer	127
13. I am Righteous	137

14. I am Set Apart	147
15. I am Valuable	157
Afterword	171
About the Author	173
Endnotes	175

Cristee' -
Thank you for your kindness, patience, love,
and unwavering support over this past year,
as I spent far too much time
in front of a computer monitor and keyboard.
A million positive adjectives wouldn't be enough
to describe all that you are to me.
Thank you.

Nate Dewberry -
"Thank you"
doesn't seem like nearly enough
to quantify the impact
you have had on my life,
but still—
Thank You.

Payton Linder -
Your emails, texts, messages, and phone calls
breathe life into my soul.
Your encouragement means
more than you know.
Thank you.
(*Go get 'em, Tiger.*)

The Redeemed -
Rarely do I have the opportunity to be a part of a ministry
that advances the Kingdom of God as powerfully as The Redeemed.
This is more than a men's ministry—it is a movement
with a true heart for bringing men closer to their Creator.
I see the impact every day, and I am honored to be a part of it.
Thank you.

ACKNOWLEDGEMENTS

I owe a special thank you to Nate Dewberry, Director of The Redeemed men's ministry. If you had never responded to my inquiry back in September of 2022, there's a good chance this book would never have been written. You are a true friend, mentor, and brother in Christ—someone who continually challenges me, encourages me, and walks alongside me on this journey called life.

I also want to recognize the Bible study group my wife and I attend. The friends we have made through this group have become family. We have laughed together, cried together, studied God's Word, prayed for one another, and even entrusted them to care for our chickens and cats while we were out of town. Tom and Sharon, Tracy and Gerry, Tom and Darla—you have become more than friends; you are family. And to our occasional VIP guests, Lee and Diane Boleyn—I can't wait to spend eternity with each of you.

There's another group of men who inspire me every day. In fact, from my perspective, these men are superheroes—they faithfully show up each new day wearing the badges of boldness, courage, faith, and trust. As I've had the privilege of leading and participating in online weekly groups, I hear about their intentional journeys to be more like Christ. Daily, they invite Christ into their lives to heal the wounds of the past. They look ahead to how they can be used by God to bring others along with them. These men are my friends, *Brothers in Christ*, and *Warriors on the Battlefield*. You are the men I look up to.

Finally, I want to acknowledge an incredible friend who has taught me so much about friendship, mentoring, and discipleship—Jarrett, you are a giant in the faith to me. I have watched you patiently walk in faith, lead with wisdom, and mentor others with humility and grace. Your love for Christ and your relentless pursuit of a deeper identity in Him inspire me daily. Thank you for the privilege of being your friend.

FORWARD

Few things are more powerful than truly understanding who we are—our identity at the deepest level. In a world filled with confusion, competing narratives, and ever-changing definitions of self-worth, Jim Miner's *Identity Revealed* is a beacon of clarity and truth. I am thrilled to introduce this remarkable book, a work born out of Jim's deep reflection, dedicated study, and unwavering commitment to living in his God-given identity. His passion for helping others grasp the profound realities of their identity in Christ radiates from every page.

This book is not merely an academic or theological discourse. It is a guide—one that will walk you through the journey of discovering, internalizing, and ultimately living out the identities God has given you. Jim does not write from a place of detached scholarship but from personal experience. He has wrestled with these truths, lived them out, and now shares them with an authenticity that makes this book not just informative but transformative.

In *Identity Revealed*, Jim tackles one of the most foundational yet often overlooked aspects of faith—our identity in Christ. So many believers go through life without ever fully realizing the inheritance, authority, and confidence that come with truly knowing who they are in God. They battle insecurity, doubt, and the lies of the enemy, never walking in the freedom and power that Christ has made available to them. Jim has a burden for those who find themselves in that struggle, and this book is his response to that need.

One of the things I appreciate most about Jim's approach is its practicality. He doesn't just offer theological insights—he equips readers with tools to apply these truths to their daily lives. Each chapter serves as both a revelation and a call to action, helping readers move from knowledge to experience. Whether you are new to the faith or have walked with God for years, this book will challenge you to examine the way you see yourself and embrace the identity God has already given you.

At its core, *Identity Revealed* is about transformation. It's about standing against the lies of the enemy and replacing them with God's truth. It's about shaking off the weight of past failures, external labels, and false narratives to walk boldly in the fullness of God's calling. As you journey through these pages, you will be reminded that your identity is not something you have to earn, achieve, or prove—it is something already established in Christ. Jim beautifully articulates this reality and provides a roadmap to help readers step into that freedom.

Reading this book will not leave you unchanged. Jim's words have a way of cutting through the noise and speaking directly to the heart. His writing is honest, compelling, and deeply rooted in scripture, making *Identity Revealed* a book that will not only inspire you but also equip you for the battles ahead. In a time when so many struggle to find their place, their purpose, and their sense of worth, this message is more crucial than ever. I am incredibly proud of Jim for undertaking this work, and I am confident that *Identity Revealed* will profoundly impact those who read it. My hope is that as you turn these pages, you will not only gain knowledge but experience a shift in your heart—a renewed confidence in who you are in Christ.

This is more than just a book; it is a tool for transformation. I am excited to see how its message will change countless lives.

Read with an open heart, and prepare to step into the fullness of your identity. Your life will never be the same.

Nate Dewberry
director | The Redeemed

INTRODUCTION

It's hard going through life when you believe both the spoken and unspoken lies about yourself, but that's what we do, right? When something is said to us or about us, we instinctively sort these words into mental compartments—some we ignore, others we dwell on, and some we bury deep within to protect ourselves. We either grow or slowly die under the weight of the lie.

Mentally, we sort these untruths into different categories: "I can brush that one off", or, "I noticed the sting of that one but I'm unsure what to do with it." There's the lie that hurts really badly but over time we've learned to take it on the chin and suppress it. Subtle lies are the worst—they stay on the perimeter, jabbing us ever so slightly, trying not to get noticed. Then, when the stress has built up so much and life explodes all around us, the curtain is ripped in two exposing the truth and now the jabbing has become a stabbing lie that puts you on the floor in tears.

Road maps are nonexistent and there is very little help as we try to navigate the world of lying because that dark realm is constantly changing. I would dare speculate that everyone, at some point in their life, has either told a lie or been told a lie. There's a very high level of probability for that speculation.

I have done my share of lying to family and friends over the years and reaped the harsh consequences. The hurt I've caused others by what I've said must have been heart-wrenching, and for that, I apologize. In return, I've believed some of the lies told to me throughout my life as well.

Here's the conundrum, regardless of the type of lie we've been told, eventually it affects our identity and that is the reason behind writing this book. The older we become, the more our identity begins to develop. Early on, the short one-liners become the foundation for what we eventually believe about ourselves, and those beliefs become our identity.

Because the topic of our identity is vast and layered, it's important to clarify what we're addressing here. Let's start with this: Have you ever thought, "I'm so deeply rooted in anxiety and depression that fear, shame, and guilt control every aspect of my life"? Or, "I'm so attached to the hurts of my past, there's no future for me"? Maybe, you might be able to resonate with this one "I've had so many people push me down there's no reason to think about trying to get back up." Some of us might even say, "You know, I'm good. My identity is solid" but behind those confident words, there might be a little boy or girl still longing to be affirmed, encouraged, or told they are valuable.

But lies don't just shape how we create our identity—they also affect our mental and emotional well-being. In today's world, where social media and technology slowly indoctrinate us into believing a false narrative—an identity we feel we must live up to. Research shows a significant increase in the number of electronics in the home. It's my theory that the phone, tablet, and/or computer have become substitutes for any real tangible relationships. We then leave it up to the programmers to shape and develop the identities of our children, and ourselves. We allow influencers to do just that, influence us.

"Children's use of mobile and interactive media has increased rapidly over the past decade. Recent estimates reveal that the majority of parents own smartphones, on which they allow their children to play games or watch videos. Up to 75% of young children have their own tablets, and infants are estimated to start handling mobile devices during the first year of life..."[1]

The question has to be presented, thought about, and discussed, "What happens when there are no longer any more influencers?" A different way of asking the question would be "How do we traverse our own personal identity when we are no longer interested in a particular influencer?"

Is our core belief based off of what others think we should be like, which will fade away, or are we basing our identity on who our Creator has defined us to be as believers in Christ, which will never fade away?

INTRODUCTION

As you read through the pages of *Identity Revealed*, think of it as a devotional invitation to explore who you are based on God's reality. Yep, you read that correctly—God's reality of who you are. The truths you will read about will challenge the way you think and perceive yourself. This book may test every introspective thought you might have but, in the end, I'm confident you will come away with a more profound understanding of your true identity which changes the way you live out your Christ-centered life.

We've been conditioned to let our feelings dictate our lives. But emotions, while important, should not define our identity. Feelings are not meant to define us, but they do reveal importance, validation, and direction. Just like the traffic signs we see every day; our feelings should help direct us to the core feelings that have gone unmet. It takes courage, faith, and trust to follow the emotional road signs of our lives. It means we go from acting to believing.

When reading books such as *Unwanted* by Jay Stringer, *Free to Thrive* by Josh McDowell and Ben Bennett, and *Atomic Habits* by James Clear, they all in some manner reference that we do not feel our way into believing, instead we believe first and then the corresponding feelings will follow. In other words, we grab ahold of the belief of our identity in Christ first, and then, the feelings will follow suit.

If you picked up this book out of curiosity as it pertains to your own true identity, it's out of the same curiosity that I wrote this book.

While growing up my family was a little disorganized which put me in the perfect place to form my own troubled belief system of "I'm not important or valuable". There were more questions than answers and it was easy to get lost in the confusion of everyday life. By the time I was a teenager, I had fully bought into the lie that I wasn't valuable. That belief led me down some really dark roads—ones I never thought I'd recover from.

In the following chapters, you will read about how my life changed at the age of nine when I accepted the Lord as my Savior. Before the altar call was given, the preacher was adamant that if you accept Christ then you will go to heaven and if you do not then you will go to hell when you die. Although, biblically, this is correct, it's sure to make a significant impression on any nine-year-old. One clarifying statement was, "Now that you've accepted Christ as your Savior, you have a golden ticket into heaven." Again, he was correct, but that's all I learned.

As I continued with my life, pastors expounded on every topic imaginable from the Bible, but I don't remember too many that specifically discussed our identity in Christ.

It's hard to share that during my formative years, I had a dad but no father. There was a presence in the house but there was no relationship between me and my dad, between me and my father. It wasn't until my early twenties that someone pointed out to me that even though I recognized who God was in my life, I didn't yet know my Heavenly Father was. That was an eye-opener for sure. At first, it was difficult to distinguish God as my Heavenly Father when the only comparison I had was to someone who had been absent in my life. As the years progressed it became easier to settle in my Father's lap and tell Him about my day.

There were more struggles and disappointments along the way that led to more wrong decisions, and then in the fall of 2022, I heard a podcast that talked about our true identity in Christ as believers. Oh my. That one message had more influence on my way of thinking than most of the sermons I've ever heard. I was blown away by the idea that my Heavenly Father saw me as Forgiven, Blessed, Confident, His Friend, and Child and I had to learn more.

The identities mentioned in this book are unchangeable, immutable, and eternal—they are God's truth, not mine. They can be relied upon day after day or year after year. Instead of trying to buy into the ever-changing and confusing culture and social media mayhem, with *Identity Revealed* you have a chance to rest in the clarity and assurance that your Heavenly Father has already provided you.

Think of the relevancy of your life whether you are looking to establish a brand-new Christ-centered relationship or if you need to build on what has already been created.

Getting my bible, journal, commentaries, and concordances out, I took out my shovel and started digging deep into numerous identities which soon became this book, *Identity Revealed*. One of the first things I did was create beautifully colored 4 x 6 cards that present an identity on the

INTRODUCTION

front and then biblical information on the back to reinforce the identity. Several of these cards are placed throughout my home to remind me every day of God's reality of who I am. You'll notice at the end of each chapter there is a QR code that, when scanned, takes you directly to an *identity* screensaver: a daily reminder of who you are in Christ. A reminder of how Your Heavenly Father sees you.

One last note...

I don't have a Ph.D. or a Master's degree, and I'm not a pastor. Outside of a B.A. degree that is no longer used, there are no other certifications hanging on my wall. I've spent time in counselors' and pastors' offices working through issues from my past and I fully understand I still have a long way to go. I recognize that every great thing in my life is solely due to God, my Heavenly Father. It has been the prompting of the Holy Spirit who has guided me on this journey of writing *Identity Revealed*. Again, all recognition for any positive impact this book may have belongs to God. My only certification is life itself, my teacher is the Holy Spirit, and my textbook is the Word of God.

For each chapter, countless hours have been put into researching that particular identity. It's been fun writing about some of my favorite memories while growing up and memories with my family as the kids were younger.

I am confident and I believe with each page turned, the details—and application of the identities in Christ—will offer a new way to think about who you are in Christ.

The chapters are easy to read, but it's the message that matters the most. It's more about the true identity we have as believers. Toward the end of each chapter, there is a section titled, Points to Ponder. This is a chapter review usually adding one or two significant points. There is also a list of questions for you to reflect on, actually, journal through if you can. Most chapters have a call to action that you'll have to check out. Again, the last thing you will see is the Identity in Christ QR screensaver codes as mentioned above.

There's no rush when reading *Identity Revealed* because learning about our true identity is a journey. Let this book be your guide. I can't wait to hear how your identity in Christ is revealed to you.

A brother in Christ

Jim

Chapter One

I AM BLESSED

*Praise be to the God and Father of our Lord Jesus Christ,
who has blessed us in the heavenly realms
with every spiritual blessing in Christ.*

Ephesians 1:3

The English language can sometimes be complicated and confusing, especially for me.

My grades in high school weren't the best, and the only thing I remember from my English class is that a verb signifies action and a noun represents a person, place, or thing—oh, and a few descriptive adjectives too. That's about the extent of my knowledge when it comes to writing. Wait, I still remember to capitalize the first letter of a sentence and end a sentence with a period... most of the time.

Because of my lack of knowledge in this area, I am very thankful that my wife majored in English while in college. Her deep understanding of sentence structure has been a tremendous help while writing this devotional study guide.

A fascinating aspect of the English language is that a single word can have multiple meanings. There's a word for this phenomenon: *polysemous*.

The word "*blessed(ing)*" in Ephesians 1:3 fits this definition because it has multiple meanings.

Over time, multiple meanings have been assigned to the word "blessed." But what does the word *blessed(ing)* mean in the context of Ephesians 1:3?

Before we can answer that question, let's become acquainted with the backstory for Ephesians. Paul wrote four books of the New Testament while under house arrest for two years in Rome: Ephesians, Philippians, Colossians, and Philemon. These four letters are called the *prison epistles*.

The church in Ephesus was especially dear to Paul because "He had lived, ministered, prayed, and fought fierce battles on behalf of those believers for more than two years."[1] However, he faced quite a dilemma. Paul wanted to go to Jerusalem for Pentecost, but he also had an intense desire to meet with the leaders from Ephesus beforehand.

It was there on the beach in Miletus, which is about 30 miles south of Ephesus, that Paul met with the church elders. But, why? What was so urgent?

It was widely known that there was a death threat against Paul. Having been a Jewish Pharisee who now shares the gospel with the Gentiles he used to persecute, he was fully aware of a plot to remove him from the picture by the Pharisees he once belonged to. Going to Rome would only intensify the Jewish Pharisaical anger towards him. Paul believed that if he didn't stop to see the church elders first, he might not get another chance because of what awaited him in Rome.

This short meeting was to encourage the elders to stand watch over their flock of believers in Ephesus just in case the Pharisees in Rome were able to carry out the plot to kill Paul. Eliminating Paul from the scene would remove one of the strongest pillars the New Testament church ever had.

Understanding Paul's background helps us grasp the weight of his words. In this chapter we will explore and gain a better appreciation for the powerful meaning behind the three different ways Paul uses the word blessed(ing) in Ephesians 1:3.

- *Blessed be*
- *Has blessed*
- *Blessing*

Keep in mind that within each of these different ways, there are distinct meanings as well. Let's take a look.

Eulogétos[1] is the Greek word for Blessed.

Don't worry, I can't pronounce it either. Here is the phonetic spelling just in case you would like to give it a try: yoo-log-ay-tos'

At first glance, we may not recognize it but we are already familiar with this Greek word.

As we continue following the breadcrumbs further down the path we can finally make the connection. The Greek verb εὐλογέω (eulogeō), means "*to bless*" or "*to speak well of.*" This root word gives us the modern English word *eulogy*.

Wait a minute!

Let that sink in.

Did that take you by surprise because it did for me?

What is the first thing that comes to your mind when you realize the phrase *blessed* means *eulogy*? If you are anything like me, I think of a funeral.

The Merriam-Webster Dictionary confirms this thought with the following definition. "A commendatory oration or writing, especially in honor of one deceased."[2] The Greek definition continues with this main thought of what we might see practiced at a funeral as we consider the memories shared by friends and family. However, as we continue to learn about this new identity, we will begin to capture the full context of *blessed* and that it can even be applied to just about any celebration of life such as weddings, promotions, or affirming a friend.

Now that we understand the Greek root of 'blessed,' let's examine how Paul uses it in context with each of the blessed(ing) references.

BLESSED BE..

This is the first time Paul uses the phrase *Blessed be* in the book of Ephesians and it's a great way to start. It is important to note this specific first step as it pertains to blessed be as presented here. Before Paul continues any further with this epistle, he recognizes the need to bless God and the Father of our Lord Jesus Christ.

Yes, we mortal humans can bless God and there are eight examples of this in the New Testament.[3]

Culturally, blessings were an important part of religious and social life. This was a way of invoking favor and expressing gratitude. It was also an integral part of worship and daily life often used to acknowledge God's sovereignty and provision.

This is a particularly descriptive word that means *'well-spoken of'* and it is used *only when referring to God*.[4] God alone is truly worthy of every "good acknowledgment"—or **eulogy**. The word **eulogy** literally means "a well-spoken word," and it's the kind of praise we can offer Him.

...HAS BLESSED...

Next, Paul focuses on this blessed expression, *"...who has blessed us..."*[5] The usage of this particular phrase infers the blessing is being directed towards those in a personal relationship with Christ. In this statement, God has already blessed His people. This is a past-tense blessing with a current-day application.

Remember, Paul has already acknowledged who is providing the blessing and what is being blessed.

The definition used here is God speaking "well of" or "blessing" us, or even "for God to cause someone to prosper, to make them happy, or to bestow blessings on."

Essentially, God is the "who" and those who believe in Christ as the Risen Savior are the ones being blessed.

...WITH EVERY SPIRITUAL BLESSING...

As mentioned above, the third application is *"...with every spiritual blessing..."*[6] and here, the focus shifts to how God directs His blessings toward believers.

The Greek word for this blessing has changed ever so slightly to *eulogia*. It is still in the same family as *eulogy* but like so many other words, this one has a new definition,

adulation [adoration], praise, blessing, gift (emphasis added)

"The word carries connotations of praise and thanksgiving, often directed towards God or as a divine favor bestowed upon individuals [believers in Christ] (emphasis added)."[7] Imagine that, as you greet someone and laughter, encouragement, or prayer ensues, you are blessing them. If you send a card, a special emoji, or take a meal to someone, you are blessing them. Sometimes a firm handshake, a warm hug, or just listening can also equate to a blessing that you are giving to someone else.

Here's one of several ways I have been blessed. A couple of years ago my wife and I were heading to an appointment in a city an hour and a half away. We arrived quite early for the appointment so we decided to grab some lunch. In the front lobby of the restaurant I saw a gentleman wearing a t-shirt that signified he was a Veteran. Occasionally, when I notice something like this, I approach the person and say, "From one Veteran to another, I'd like to thank you for your service." A firm handshake usually ensues and we both stand a little taller.

The waitress walked my wife and I back to our table where we enjoyed a great conversation and meal. Once the waitress dropped the ticket off at our table, we began to get ready to head out for the appointment. Suddenly, without any notice, a man that overheard the conversation with the Veteran in the lobby, came to our table and asked, "Did I hear you say you were a Veteran?" Proudly, I acknowledged that I was and immediately this very robust man grabbed our ticket and said, "I would like to thank you for your service by paying for your meal."

That blessing set the tone for my wife and me for the rest of the day. As a matter of fact, I have shared that story with several of my friends who are Veterans and they were just as amazed at this blessing as I was.

By separating these three blessed(ing)'s, we explored the meaning behind each one. Now it's time to bring all three uses of 'blessed' back together, just as Paul originally intended, so we can identify the spiritual gifts he describes.

In Ephesians 1:3-14, Paul lists eight spiritual blessings, all which reflect God's intentional generosity toward us.

1. Chosen before time and the creation of the universe (v. 4).

2. Predestined for adoption (vs. 5)

3. Accepted in Christ (vs. 6)

4. Redeemed and Forgiven (vs. 7)

5. Given knowledge of God's mysteries (vs. 9)

6. Promised an eternal inheritance (vs. 11)

7. Sealed with the Holy Spirit (vs. 13)

8. Guaranteed eternal redemption (vs. 14)

Today, as a believer in Christ, you can say,

I am Blessed

POINTS TO PONDER

We've learned the root word for blessed(ing) used in Ephesians 1:3 means eulogy. At first, it sounds awkward because we connect eulogy with funerals. Yet, for the believer, a funeral is a time for celebration where we recognize the life of the person who has passed away has blessed us. Accordingly, this is a time when we bless that person with our favorite memories of how that family member or friend blessed us.

How does the idea that 'blessing' means 'eulogy' change your understanding of what it means to bless God and others?

The first *blessed* refers to believers appreciating God's divine nature and reverence. Write down a few familiar attributes of God and then explain how you can actively acknowledge and bless him this week (1 Chronicles 29:10-13).

The second *blessed* is God blessing those who believe in him. Even within this verse we are studying, Ephesians 1:3, we can be reminded that through our faith in Christ, we are adopted, redeemed, and have an eternal inheritance. Describe a couple of blessings God has granted you and why they are so special.

The third blessing has two meanings with the first being how we can bless others and the second being that God still blesses us with spiritual gifts. Paul describes in 2 Corinthians 9:8-11 the importance of blessing others because of how God has blessed us. Then in 1 Corinthians 12:4-7 Pauls describes how God blesses the believers with spiritual gifts. Reflect on a time when you blessed someone else. What was the occasion? What was the blessing you gave? Describe the impact it had on the other person(s).

Name a few blessings God has given you. Why do they stand out in your life?

Within the first 14 verses of Ephesians, Chapter 1, Paul wrote down eight different spiritual blessings every believer in Christ is afforded. Which one(s) do you connect with the most and why is it so important to you?

Write down a few action steps that will allow you to purposefully and intentionally apply this Identity to your life.

I am Blessed Screen Saver

Chapter Two

I AM CHOSEN

*But you are a chosen people,
a royal priesthood,
a holy nation,
God's special possession,
that you may declare the praises of him
who called you out of darkness into his wonderful light.*

1 Peter 2:9

Who knew that allowing one man into a boat could be so life-changing? But that's exactly what happened.

News about Jesus was spreading throughout the region. He was gaining popularity and oftentimes, where he went, people went. They were eager to hear him impart wisdom, tell stories, and share more parables.

Jesus had amassed quite a few followers who wanted to hear him speak, and on this particular day, they were pressing in from all sides. As the crowd grew, they became tighter and tighter, forcing him to the water's edge, where the waves of the Sea of Galilee were lapping at his feet.

Jesus was teaching the Word of God, and the people were hungry for it.

Seeing two boats nearby, Jesus stepped into one, which was owned by Andrew and Simon, who was also known as Peter.

Have you ever wondered if Jesus stepped into that fishing boat for his safety from the crowd — or was there an underlying plan?

On this specific day in Jesus' life, he never needed to worry about his safety, so we can count that out as to why he stepped into the boat.

Think about it, though. What were all the individual conditions that had to have happened for Jesus to step into Peter's boat? It makes you a little curious, doesn't it?

Peter and Andrew were ordinary fishermen, returning from a routine fishing trip — having caught nothing the night before. The frustration must have been high. They had done everything they were taught and gone to all the best fishing spots, only to come up empty-handed.

Defeated.

Other fishermen returned with their usual haul but not these two. As men who had spent years perfecting their craft, they were defeated.

Nothing.

The incredible effort they put into the only profession they knew resulted in absolutely nothing.

Ridiculed.

Not only were their nets empty, but now they had to face the ridicule of the other fishermen nearby—the guys they grew up with, friends, and peers. Sure, there may have been the usual bantering going back and forth, but this cut deeper — it reflected on them and the trade they had devoted their whole lives to.

I imagine Jesus was in the bow of the boat while speaking to the crowd, and Peter and Andrew were in the stern. Unlike the crowd that pressed into Jesus, these two brothers had somewhat of a front-row seat, well, more of a back-row seat, while listening to the Master teach. They could not abandon ship and swim to shore; it was their boat. Staying and listening was the only option, and it turned out to be a good one.

Then, something happened.

Something that would change their lives forever.

Jesus was done speaking and the crowd was heading back to whatever their day held for them, but not so much for Peter and Andrew. Jesus knew what he was doing as he slowly turned to the back of the fishing boat now looking directly at the two brothers.

Fear.

Excitement.

Curiosity.

What were they feeling at this very moment?
Exhausted from the night before they must have been taken aback when they heard Jesus tell them to turn their boats around and head back out to the deep part of the sea.
"Nope."
"Not going to do it."
Those could have been the first thoughts between these two.
Then, Peter submitted to the request stating the following,
"Master, because it is you who asked, we will do as you commanded."
I'm wondering if it was the way Jesus told them to head back out or was there such a compassionate look in his eyes that it could not be ignored?
Nonetheless, they did as they were commanded.

Doubt.

"The fish aren't going to bite."
"You're the teacher—we're the fishermen. We know what we're doing. You don't."
Could these have been the thoughts of two strong-willed fishermen who were going to be humbled by the Lord?
Christ knew the exact spot where the fish were swimming.
"Here.
This is the spot.
Now, let down your nets and catch fish."

Bewilderment.

The two brothers must have given each other the look. The look that carries with it a multitude of thoughts.

"Why didn't he have us take him back to shore when he was done teaching?"

"This is not going to work."

Tug.

"What was that?"
"It's just a figment of our imagination."

Pull.

"There it goes again."

Splash.

The calm surface of the water is now interrupted by the splashing of fish filling up the nets. Silver scales and fins are crashing over each other as the boat now begins to lean closer to the surface of the sea.

Excitement.

The yelling begins.
"Grab this. Grab that."
"How is this happening?"
The weight of the fish threatened to sink their boat.

As the two brothers yelled for help from the other boat nearby, they looked back to see Jesus sitting there amid all this commotion, smiling.

Realization.

Peter thought he was just a fisherman. But in that moment, he realized he had been chosen for something greater. Like Peter, we often define ourselves by our circumstances — but Jesus sees more. He calls us into a greater purpose, just as he called Peter.

"When Simon Peter saw this, he fell at Jesus' knees and said, "Go away from me, Lord; I am a sinful man!" [1]

I AM CHOSEN

Peter, the know-it-all fisherman, became a humbled, sinful man at Jesus feet in his own boat, which was in utter pandemonium in the middle of the sea. Has that ever happened to you? Life is swirling all around you and it feels completely out of control and then the Holy Spirit taps you on the shoulder with an idea, a thought, a new passion. In the middle of all the chaos, God chooses you for something that only you can lead or support. Because of your history, obedience, or faithfulness, God, through the Holy Spirit, starts the nudging process for a particular kingdom mission.

"Then He said to them, "Follow Me, and I will make you fishers of men." Matthew 4:19

There it is, the calling. The Choosing.

On that eventful day, Jesus *chose* Peter and Andrew to follow him — and their lives changed forever. This choice resulted in a calling to become a fisher of men for the kingdom of God. This choosing, this calling wasn't just for them. It's for us too.

Remember, God does not choose people by happenstance. Before the beginning of time, God already had a plan for each one of us. A plan to be in a relationship with him and advance his kingdom.

You might think, well, "I'm not qualified to do anything." Or, "I don't know how to do..." Here is one of my favorite excuses of why we think we cannot do something, "But, you don't know my past." Maybe so, but God does.

We need to understand this election automatically comes with an equipping. For some of us, the implementation of the plan happens immediately because we have already been trained or have experience in a specific situation or area. For others, the calling happens with education, training, or mentoring becoming a part of the call.

"You did not choose me, but I chose you and appointed you so that you might go and bear fruit – fruit that will last – and so that whatever you ask in my name the Father will give you." John 15:16

It is important to note, this was not just an everyday type of calling; it was a directive. Jesus was not asking these two brothers to check their schedule to see if they could fit him in for coffee and donuts. There was no asking if they wanted to follow him, it was instead a message to them that there is work in God's kingdom that needs to be done right now.

On what was supposed to be an ordinary day for Peter and Andrew, instead it turned out to be something that was life-changing. While finishing up on the night shift at work and getting ready to head home, when a whirlwind of unexpected activity swirled around them. Second-guessing themselves, an unusual guest, nets full of fish, boats close to sinking, and then came a calling and a choice.

I can relate to Peter and Andrew when they were repairing their nets from an unproductive night and they had to listen to the bantering, teasing, and ridicule from the other fishermen. They just wanted to be left alone and drown in their sorrows.

Peter thought he was a fisherman, but Jesus saw something more. How often do we limit ourselves, believing we're not qualified or chosen? I've felt that way too.

When I was in elementary school, I was the kid chosen last for most of the activities, especially when it came to sports. I'm guessing the black-framed glasses with the Coke-bottle-thick lenses and my social awkwardness put a target on my back that read, "Nerd." Besides, nerds don't play sports. In fact, they barely watch sports at all. Well, at least from my standpoint.

In years past, I've asked myself too many times, why couldn't I have been chosen as one of the first 29 students instead of the 30th? Dodgeball, volleyball, basketball, why was I always the last to be picked. As of today, I have no clearer answer than before.

Name-calling was another fun activity for the other kids on the playground because I was the one being called names. The bantering, teasing, and ridicule were relentless at times and it hurt.

Can you identify with being chosen last or teased and ridiculed? Have you ever wanted to disappear into the night believing no one would ever notice? I get it. That's a tough part of life for anyone to walk away from, but I can tell you from experience there is hope.

In Christ, you're no longer just picked — you're completely Chosen, just like Peter and Andrew.

On the day Jesus chose Peter and his brother, I'm guessing their self-esteem levels were drastically low. For me, being chosen last and putting up with all the name-calling tanked my self-esteem as well.

When I was 9 years old, I made a huge decision that would change my life forever. Under a huge canvas tent filled with over a hundred kids, when the altar call was given, I accepted Christ into my heart at Bible camp. That was the day Jesus slowly turned to me and in the most tender way possible, reached his hand out to mine and asked if I would like to walk with him.

I grabbed his hand and would not let go.

That is the day of choosing. Jesus chose me and I chose him.

Is it possible that some of you reading this book can relate to Peter's story? To my story?

While growing up you may have been the last kid to be picked. Or, maybe, you were never included in any of the other reindeer games. The words you heard were more like rocks, knives, and spears that cut to your heart so sharply. For a while, you were wounded and discarded. There was so much doubt and bewilderment in your life that you questioned what the next minute would bring.

Splash.

Could you even keep your head above water?

Even though my Heavenly Father already had a plan in place for my life, it wasn't until decades later that I began to fully understand that on that late afternoon at Bible camp, God was looking down at me saying, "That one. You. You're mine and I want to impact your life forever. Today, I choose you."

On that day God gave me additional gifts that I didn't open until much later in my life. For whatever reason it wasn't until 50-plus years later that

1 Peter 2:9 began to come alive in my heart. When I was nine years old, I had already developed a negative understanding of being chosen. Now, in this stage of my life, I am no longer the last person who was picked.

I am Chosen.

CHOSEN MEANS...

When Peter was writing his first book, he used the Greek word *eklektos*, which translates into our English word for chosen and it carries with it the following definition,

Those chosen out by God for the rendering of special service to Him.[2]

And this Greek word looks a lot like the word elect. That's because elect is another root word meaning,

chosen from, out of, especially as a deeply personal choice.[3]

This choice by God is drastically opposite from what social media has conditioned us to believe. When scrolling through hundreds if not thousands of social media posts, and without any consideration as to what was posted, we quickly pick, or "like" what we just saw. There is very little thought that goes into a "thumbs up" or "thumbs down" emoji. We have now been trained to make an instantaneous decision that has no lasting quality to it whatsoever. Whereas, when being chosen, there is a deliberate and concise decision being made. A decision that could potentially have lasting implications.

When God chooses someone, he takes time to consider how this person will reflect the sovereign and special relationship the two of them can have. There is a special purpose or destiny assigned to those God chooses.

THERE'S MORE

Peter doesn't just stop with the identity of being chosen, he continues by adding

"*a royal priesthood,*

a holy nation..."
and
"*...for God's own possession.*"
Here is an overview of each of these additional identities.
"*...a royal priesthood...*"[4]
The combined meaning here describes a characteristic of royalty, and that royalty is set apart to serve God.

For this next phrase, we recognize this as believers, that we are set apart for God's holy purpose.
"*...a holy nation...*"[5]
Lastly,
"*... for God's own possession.*"
which means we are God's treasure, cherished and protected.[6]
In this one verse, 1 Peter 2:9, there are four identities we can claim,
I am Chosen
I am a Royal Priest
I am a Set Apart
I am God's Treasure

Accepting and walking in the above-mentioned identities is a visible sign of faith and obedience within our relationship with Christ. We are purposefully and intentionally putting our old lives on the altar, sacrificing it and putting it behind us.

THE CALLING

There is another important piece to this verse that we need to follow up with. Well, it's more of a responsibility believers have been given.

Just like Peter and Andrew who were chosen first and then called, the same holds fast to each believer. We have been called
"*...to proclaim the virtues of Him who called you...*"[7]

The New International Version says it a little differently, "*...that you may declare the praises of him who called you...*" And the New Living Translation says it this way, "*As a result, you can show others the goodness of God...*"

We are to be an example for God through moral excellence, strength, and righteousness.

POINTS TO PONDER

Even though this verse presents us with several new identities in Christ, they all come with a calling. Jesus called Peter and Andrew to become fishers of men and he has called you and me to proclaim what he has done in our lives. How he has removed us from the darkness into his marvelous light, his presence.

You may have been picked last in the world's eyes, but in God's eyes, you were chosen first. Now, how will you walk in that calling today?

The names you were called as a kid cannot even compare to the new identities God has freely given you. If that happened to you, I'm sure it was and maybe still is a difficult time for you. What is your definition of "picked" versus "chosen?" Does it line up with what you read earlier? Why or why not?

List out a couple of ways you were "picked" for something. Were you the first one picked, or the last one?

At what point in your life did you fully understand your new identity in Christ, "I am Chosen?"

What does knowing you are part of a Royal Priesthood, a Holy Nation, and God's Treasured Possession mean to you?

The last part of this verse says that we are to proclaim, as a Chosen people, how God has brought us out of a sinful life into his marvelous presence. Identify at least three people you can pray for and begin to share your "Chosen" story with.

Write down a few action steps that will allow you to purposefully and intentionally apply this Identity to your life.

I am Chosen Screensaver

Chapter Three

I AM COMPLETE

And in Christ you have been brought to fullness...

Colossians 2:10

The year 2022 was absolutely crazy for my wife and me. At least that's the word my wife used—"crazy". For me, it was intense, stressful, and filled with so much anxiety I thought I was going to step off the nearest curb.

You see, we are empty nesters and thought we needed a few projects to keep us busy. Our idea of "a few" definitely didn't match the actual definition.

Let me explain...

My wife had dreamed of building a brand-new home on farmland passed down to her through her family. For her, this was at least 15 years in the making. She is the country girl who finds peace in living in the rolling hills of NE Iowa. For me, at the time — not so much. I am the big city boy. I have lived in huge metropolitan cities all my life and I was not sure giving that up was a good thing.

There's a certain vibe and energy only big cities can produce. The lights, sounds, and people are all amazing. It's fast-paced with everything moving a hundred miles an hour.

My image of living in the country was sitting on the front porch watching the corn grow. Now I am sure that is a lot of fun for some people, like farmers, but not so much for me.

I had severe reservations about building our retirement home an hour and a half away outside of a big city and downsizing to a town with a population of 204. That's why it took my wife all of 15 years to convince me it was a good idea.

So, that is how 2022 started.

We found a general contractor, designed our house plans, and got to work in February.

One month later, in March, our oldest son was married to his wonderful bride and we gained a daughter (in-law).

The weather finally began to cooperate and in April we broke ground in the dense clay soil where our home would soon stand. That is also the time I began to fully understand we were not embarking on a "few" projects. While my wife was working the 9 to 5 gig, I stayed home, managing most of the projects swirling around us.

We were at the nearest home improvement store picking out paint colors, light fixtures, and faucets for our new home seemingly every day. At the same time, though, we realized we also had to choose paint colors and new carpet for our current home that we had to get ready to put on the market. There were days a 30-minute trip to the big box store turned into several hours.

Then we noticed it.

The interlocking flooring in the kitchen of the home we needed to sell began showing signs of what turned out to be a significant problem. The planks were bubbling at the seams and we both knew right away that meant water damage. We got the flashlight out and began looking everywhere for water leaks but we found nothing.

Where was the water coming from?

There it was. Hiding right in front of our eyes.

The back wall under the kitchen sink looked different and a simple touch of the drywall gave way to creating a hole the size of our fist. The drywall was soft and mushy. The more we removed it, the more we realized the kitchen sink drain pipe was the culprit. The house was built in the late

1960s and galvanized plumbing was the ideal choice. However, this pipe had corroded so much you could see 2" – 3" holes where the water was leaking down the inside wall and under the flooring.

It became evident that we were not only building a brand-new home, but now we had to make the hard decision to gut the kitchen down to the bare bones and start from scratch.

Frustration set in as we added one more project to our already growing list.

Now we had to buy all new plumbing, cabinets, and finishes—for a kitchen we wouldn't even use.

Ugh. This was not in our original plans.

More decisions to make at the home improvement store. More calls to find different contractors for our current home while managing the contractors for our new home.

When will all this be done?

When will this be complete?

Oh, and I had to relocate my photography business—three counties away?

Let's not forget the 8-day, 7-night cruise we had to take or we would lose significant cruise credits, aka, money.

The kitchen remodel was finally complete. We sold our home in about two weeks and went on our cruise.

Two things completed. But wait, there's more to add to the list.

Now it was just a matter of packing a 3-bedroom home into an undersized U-Haul—that was my fault. My wife suggested the large truck but I assured her the smaller one would be just fine.

I remember the day we started packing up the U-Haul truck to move from our old home to the new one. It was November 19, 2022. We had a great team of friends and family playing Tetris with all our furniture and boxed-up belongings. Once the truck was filled, I got in the cab, turned the key, and made the right-hand turn out of the driveway so I could now drive that hour and a half, in a blizzard, to start unpacking everything in our new home.

Another major milestone checked off the list.

In December of that year, the bank considered our home completed and the new mortgage had to start. And just like that, our new mortgage kicked in.

That first night in our new home, as my wife and I drifted off to sleep, I finally exhaled—everything was complete.

We made it.

We're done.

No more overwhelming events to worry about. As far as I was concerned, all projects for 2022 were completed. Mind you, I said the 2022 projects were done—not the life long goals, like eventually writing a book.

In that year, we did it. We completed everything on our list.

We triumphed over our to-do list.

From my perspective, in 2022, there were millions of little decisions that built upon each other. At the end of one decision, we would check it off the to-do list as completed and then move on to the next. Eventually, everything on the list was done or completed.

Looking back, I realized something deeper. Just like our home projects, I treated my spiritual life like a never-ending checklist — constantly trying to 'finish' something. But in Christ, I was already complete. My worth wasn't tied to what I accomplished but to what He had already done.

It was only when I began studying the concept of being complete that I realized, just as each item mentioned above was checked off the to-do list, in God's eyes, I was already made complete.

For most of 2022, I was so consumed by the to-do list that I forgot who I was in Christ: complete. It was more important for me to draw a line through another task calling it complete than it was taking care of my own spiritual identity.

I AM COMPLETE

Great. I'm complete.

Now what does that really mean?

Projects get completed. The dishes get done, or completed. Homework gets completed.

But, what does it mean for us as people to be completed?

On the surface, we might feel contentment or satisfaction with our current lives. Perhaps we experience a sense of connection with others or personal fulfillment after achieving specific goals. These situations, and others like them, can give us a feeling of completeness. While this is an adequate summary, I believe that being complete is more than just a feeling.

The phrase *"... made complete..."* from Colossians 2:10 carries a significantly different meaning than the satisfaction we might have within a social group of friends or family. For those who have a personal relationship with Christ the actionable verb "...made complete..." turns from a feeling to an immutable truth and can never be taken away or changed.

to fill, to make full – it conveys the idea of filling something to its full capacity or bringing something to completion[1]

That definition would fall in line with my wife and I checking off all the boxes on our to-do list.

To fill to individual capacity.

Whereas this second definition speaks directly about an individual being filled to capacity with something.

Paul wrote this letter to the believers in the Colossian church while he was under house arrest in Rome. Controversial false teachers were trying to convince members of this young church to follow Jewish law. Paul countered by teaching that it is not what we do on the outside that matters, but what God has done on the inside, in our hearts. Because our hearts are filled to capacity with Christ, we become a visual representation for others to witness.

FILLED

Let's say that you've invited me over to your house for coffee and as we begin talking about the topic of being complete, I find the cabinet that hides the glasses and I take two of them out, placing them on the counter. As I look back in your direction I see a quizzical look on your face. "What is this guy doing?" is the message I get? After turning on the cold water from the tap, I take one glass and fill it all the way to the top. It's completely full and I can't add any more water to it. I set the glass back on the counter.

Now it's your turn.

You take the second glass and put water in it, then place the glass next to mine.

How much water did you put in the glass? Was it only filled a fourth of the way? Maybe a third of the way. For some of you, the glass was filled three-fourths of the way. And maybe a few of you filled your glass all the way to the top.

Here's my premise in this unscientific study: The first glass which is filled represents God's view of us as complete while the second glass represents how we see ourselves, through our eyes.

Think about it for a moment, the glass that is full shows us that on the day we accepted Christ into our lives, he immediately filled us up completely. He didn't look at some of us and say, "I'll only fill that person a quarter of the way because they have more sin in their life than others." Or, "That person has been really good over the years helping people so I think I will fill them up to the three-fourths line."

That's just not how it works.

How about we personalize this just a bit?

When you added water to the second glass, did old doubts come to mind? The ones telling you that you're not good enough to be complete in Christ? Because of your past, did you think God could never completely fill you up? I've been there way too often. For far too long I believed the horrible things I've said or done disqualified me to be complete in Christ.

If you didn't fill the glass to the rim, to overflowing, do you think there might be a reason?

Does anything specific come to mind?

Did you notice that within the definition of *made complete*, nothing was mentioned about only being filled a fourth of the way or half of the way? The factual definition stated, "You are complete in Him — filled to maximum capacity."

As a believer in Christ, He is the one who has Redeemed you and has *filled* you *to capacity*.

There's no exception.

No debate.
No questioning this.
It is factual and it is the truth.

THERE IS A CAVEAT

We talked about it briefly earlier in this chapter. To be made complete, it must be within a relationship with Jesus Christ, our Savior. This filling up, being complete in Him, *"belongs to all who are united to the Lord Jesus Christ."*

"...that you may be filled to the measure of all the fullness of God." Ephesians 3:19

"...who has blessed us in the heavenly realms with every spiritual blessing in Christ." Ephesians 1:3

"...to grasp how wide and long and high and deep is the love of Christ." Ephesians 3:18

"It is because of him that you are in Christ Jesus, who has become for us wisdom from God – that is, our righteousness, holiness and redemption." 1 Corinthians 1:30

Within these four short verses, there is a progression: 1) we are filled with the fullness of God, 2) who has blessed us with spiritual blessings, 3) so we can grasp the totality of Christ's love, and 4) it's because our Heavenly Father loved us so much that He sent His only Son to die for us, to forgive us of our sins. Therefore, this act of forgiveness has made us complete in righteousness, holiness, and redemption.

POINTS TO PONDER

Struggling with the tapes in our head or reliving the old memories of all the things we have said and done that were "bad" only leads to an extremely difficult day. I could create a list of all the reasons why we think we do not deserve to be fully complete in Christ but why?

About those old tapes, scripture has given us clear directions on how to handle them.

"We demolish arguments and every pretension that sets itself up against the knowledge of God, and we take captive every thought to make it obedient to Christ." [2]

The next time you have a to-do list and items are getting checked off as done, remember, as a believer, you are complete.

From now on, every time you fill a glass of water, let it remind you: You are already full in Christ. You lack nothing. You don't need to strive or prove yourself — because He has already called you complete. Change your perspective from what was to what is, and say to yourself

I am Complete!

Were you able to connect with the statement, "The list was being completed, not us" when reflecting on the story of my wife and I moving? What's the difference between completing a task off of a to-do list versus being made complete in Christ?

During the object lesson of putting water into the glass, how much water did you put in the glass and why?

Is it easy to accept this new identity—I am Complete—or do thoughts from the past still keep you from living as someone fully complete in Christ?

What additional thoughts do you have regarding being made complete within a relationship with Jesus Christ? Remember, this is not a feeling, this is a new way of believing fully in what Christ has already done for you.

Write down a few action steps that will allow you to purposefully and intentionally apply this Identity to your life.

I am Complete Screensaver

Chapter Four

I AM CONFIDENT

*Being confident of this,
that he who began a good work in you
will carry it on to completion until the day of Christ Jesus.*

Philippians 1:6

When I think about this particular identity, a specific visual picture comes to mind.

Do you remember the climactic war scene at the end of *Avengers: Endgame*? In that scene, all of the most important Avengers have been beaten down in every way imaginable. They're lying on the ground with blood, mud, and debris all around them – defeated. Then the camera slowly pans over and brings Captain America into focus. He's on his knees, exhausted, dirty, and unsure he can take his next breath, let alone stand to his feet.

But slowly and painfully, he stands to his feet.

Dark clouds and an alien spaceship loom overhead, blocking out the sun. There is very little light shining on the carnage laid out everywhere.

The camera slowly moves into position, showing Cap looking down at what was supposed to be an indestructible shield, to something that is now being held together by hope and a prayer. The shield, his shield, America's shield, has been all but destroyed, leaving only the bottom half for Cap to protect himself with. Thanos, the tyrannical villain, ripped his shield to shreds, leaving our hero defenseless and vulnerable.

We see the worn-out leather straps of his shield wrapped around his left forearm. He yanks the weathered straps that hold the shield to his arm so hard you could almost hear it snap. Tightening it down to the last notch, he's getting ready for another round with Thanos and the vast army of evildoers who are still gathering on the battlefield.

In the most dramatic way possible, Captain America slowly turns to face Thanos. He is standing alone, standing strong. It is no longer an immense army of destruction against Earth's mightiest heroes. It's now pure evil preparing to rush on one man who is not willing to give up his ground, his beliefs, or his values.

The tension is building as Cap is standing alone in his dirtied and ripped red, white, and blue superhero suit. He is representing all that is true and good. This one man is a pure example of strength, determination, and confidence.

He's digging deep on this one because he knows what is ultimately at stake.

His feet are firmly planted in the dirt, and his shoulders are squared off to face his enemies. The shield that once was a strong defensive weapon is now broken and in complete disrepair. Captain America holds it high, but it does little to protect him.

Captain America is now eye-to-eye with the leader of an army of destruction and he is unwilling to be intimidated.

This is the highest level of Confidence possible in my humble opinion.

While we love watching heroes rise in movies, real life doesn't come with a scripted victory. Many of us have felt just like Captain America—alone, weary, and overwhelmed by battles that seem impossible to win. But what if confidence wasn't about standing alone but about standing in Christ?

I could speculate that many of you reading this devotional have experienced intense situations in your lives, if not yet, you will.

Have you ever felt like you were in a movie scene similar to the one Captain America faced? But for reality's sake, let's remove the lights, cameras, costumes, and make-up. The cast, crew, and director are gone too. It's just you and life standing there *mano a mano*. It's a different type of face-off. This time, there's no popcorn or Junior Mints to get you through the scene.

Sometimes, in our daily lives, because of the stress, frustration, deadlines, finances, family, work, and so many other obstacles in our lives, it feels like we get pushed down, kicked around, and spit out for the garbage man to collect.

Maybe right now, life feels overwhelming. The weight of months—maybe years—of struggle is pressing in on you.

It's overwhelming, right?

You feel like you are on a battlefield, tired, disoriented, and confused.

How do you even think about breathing, let alone trying to stand when there are chains of an addiction, abuse, or trauma tightly cutting off all the air to your lungs? The bills are not getting paid because there is no money in your bank account. The kids are clamoring for your attention as the divorce lawyer wants to get paid for the work they have done to finalize the separation between you and what was supposed to have been your best friend.

Do you feel that sense of desperation—like Captain America? Are you down on your hands and knees, struggling to just take your next breath? Do you need to stand, but feel you lack the strength to do so?

But you must do it.

Stand.

Confident.

WHAT DOES IT MEAN?

Here is a list of synonyms for the word Confident as listed in the Merriam-Webster Dictionary,

self-assured, self-confident, self-asserting[1]

That's quite a list. If this list was the only thing I believed in, I would be the epitome of Captain America.

Did you notice anything particular about the phrases listed? They all focus on "self". Each one conveys to me that if I want to be confident, then I must be *self*-assured, *self*-reliant, and believe in *myself*. The pressure is put on me to somehow manufacture these qualities on my own. Looking at the big picture, it just seems like a never-ending loop of craziness so I can be more confident.

I'm exhausted just from thinking about it.

Please, don't get me wrong. Each of these qualities is very important, and many of us operate in this kind of confidence daily.

Every day we hear these messages in some form or another telling us who we are supposed to be or become. Some might read this list and see the image of an Alpha, Type A personality, while others look through the list of adjectives and think, "I could never measure up to any of them." The bottom line here is that these are phrases from the world's standards.

Would you be interested in seeing a list that provides freedom from what the world demands? A completely different directory that conveys a deeper sense of who we are in Christ as confident believers?

When examining the root word, *peithó*, which is the word *confident* translated into Greek, we see the following list, or phrases, that help identify the true meaning of being confident.

to persuade, assure, convince, listen, obey, and trust[2]

Going one step further, we find the root word of *peithó* is *pistis,* which has the following synonyms or phrases.

faith, which is always a gift from God, and never something that can be produced by people or moral conviction, but has a special reliance upon Christ for salvation[3]

That is quite a contrast from the first list of synonyms, isn't it? The former list had us focusing on ourselves to muster the strength to make it through each day, while the latter list shows us the confidence we have to make it through each day, which comes from *a reliance (faith) in Christ.*

As we journey deeper into our relationship with Christ, He gives us faith to rely on Him for all our needs. We rely on Him for the faith He gives us, and then we see the miraculous ways He works in our lives. It doesn't mean everything becomes perfect, it just means He is here with us, in the battle, giving us faith.

Faith to breathe.

Faith to stand.

Faith to look life straight on and declare, "God's got this."

Faith to be Confident.

"Whoever can be trusted with very little can also be trusted with much..." (Luke 16:10)

Here is another way of looking at this:

"In short, confidence, which means faith for the believer, is 'God's divine persuasion' – and therefore distinct from human confidence..."[4]

Hopefully, that's not too confusing. Let's break it down. Philippians 1:6 starts with,

"...being confident of this..."

What if we looked at it this way, we are accepting the faith God gives us, of which we can then walk through the difficult parts of our life, placing that faith back in Christ, where it belongs?

You see, confidence comes from man's ideas about the state we are in whereas faith is a gift that comes from God. Right here, at the beginning of Philippians 1:6, we have a choice to make. Do we take on the weight of a self-imposed worldly definition, or do we look to our Heavenly Father, asking him for the faith we need to navigate through the plan he has for us?

WHO?

The next thing we need to examine is who we are to have faith "in"?

The next section of this verse answers this question for us, "*...He* who began a good work in you..."

Okay, so who is the "He"?

HE is...

God, the Creator of the heavens and earth.

"I AM" THAT "I AM"

Jesus Christ, our Savior and Redeemer:

I AM the bread of life...

I AM the light of the world...

I AM the door...

I AM the good shepherd...

I AM the resurrection and the life...

I AM the way, the truth, and the life...

I AM the true vine...

Our Advocate and Comforter...

This great "I AM" is where our faith comes from.
The faith to face the next challenge.
The faith to call on those who have our backs.
    Steve Rogers, standing confident as Captain America, is in a death match with Thanos, and he is all alone. There is no one around him. Then, much to his surprise, he hears in his earpiece, "Steve..., to your left..., Cap, look to your left." Then it happens, hundreds, if not thousands, of superheroes begin to appear. They come from throughout the galaxy and multiverse to stand confidently with Captain America. Within a few short

moments, Steve Rogers is flanked on both his left and right sides by some of the strongest heroes ever.

Talk about a confidence booster. At the very last moment, when defeat is staring you directly in the face and about to throw down the hammer, your Avengers show up.

Your Avengers, if I may carefully compare, are your closest friends who really know you —those in your small group or Sunday School class at church. Maybe the men's group, college ministry, or singles group. Gather your superheroes around you for such a time as this.

As you use the faith Christ has given you to stand in the difficult moments, your faith increases and you become *confident* not in yourself but in the Great I AM THAT I AM, the bread of life…, the light of the world…, the door…, the good shepherd…, the resurrection, and the life…, the way, the truth, and the life…, the true vine…, and your Advocate and Comforter, the Holy Spirit.

How can you not begin to breathe, to get off your knees, and finally stand to face the strongholds that have bound you for so long, all because you know God is for you?

Placing the faith (confidence) that God has given you, back in Him and His plan for your life means God's "good work" will begin to be played out in your life.

It would be cool to have characters in the likes of Thor, Iron Man, Black Widow, and Spider-Man come to your aid, but you have someone even mightier than them, the Creator of the World. He is the one who breathed life into your very being. You have Jesus Christ who died on the cross for every sin you ever committed, just committed, or will commit, and you have the Holy Spirit living in you as an Advocate and Comforter in difficult times.

That's your team.
That's your crew.

That's your support system.

Today, amid whatever chaos you might be going through, take a moment to stop and close your eyes. Slowly breathe in and slowly breathe out.

Envision God, Jesus Christ, and the Holy Spirit working something good in you. Some things in you will be perfected while you are still down here on this planet while other things will be made complete when we arrive home to be in His presence.

Here are a few examples of others who have stood confident, facing their enemies or struggles in life.

David faced Goliath – 1 Samuel 17

Joshua marching around the walls of Jericho – Joshua 5:13 – 6:27

The Apostle Paul, as he was shipwrecked, beaten, and imprisoned – throughout the New Testament

I recently mentioned this statement to a friend, "God would not have placed Goliath in front of David unless he knew David could handle it."[5] God already knew when and where that battle was going to take place. He had already prepared David for this face-off. David refused to listen to the insults coming from both armies and instead went into a battle based on the confidence and faith that could only come from God. God gave David the faith to stand before a giant, and David honored God by acting on that faith—by stepping forward in full confidence.

God already knows your battles, when and where they will take place, and he is already with you, giving you the faith you need to stand strong in the Lord.

Can you stand a little taller now, not because of your strength, but as a believer Christ is in you?

Instead of focusing on the problem, focus on the One who walks with you through it. Confidence isn't about standing alone—it's about standing with the One who has already won the battle.

Stand.

Be confident.

Not in yourself – that is the way of the world.

Stand confident in what Christ is doing in your life. Stand and announce to the world,

I am Confident.

POINTS TO PONDER

Back in 2007, market research firm Yankelovich ran a survey of 4,110 people and found out that an average person sees up to 5,000 adverts every day. Today, that number is even higher, and the average person sees around 10,000 ads per day...[6] Depending on your geographical location, that may seem a little high, but that's potentially 10,000 different ways other people are telling us who we should be.

Remember the list of synonyms from the beginning of this chapter? That's those 10,000 ads per day. Remember the definition of *confident*? Focus on this one description of who you are in Christ, I am Confident, instead of the 10,000. Renew your faith in Christ, stand confident in the relationship Christ wants to have with you and watch the plans he has for you come to fruition.

Describe a moment when you were caught up in the whirlwind of the world's definition of confidence. Feel free to go back and review the list at the beginning of the chapter.

Describe a time when you were able to readily accept the faith God had given you and how you were able to walk that out in your life.

Are there any differences between these two moments you wrote down?

List three ways you can realistically live out the identity of I am Confident in your daily life by applying Matthew 17:20.

Take a look at these two verses and write down how they apply to the identity I am Confident: 2 Kings 6:16-17; Matthew 17:20

Write down a few action steps that will allow you to purposefully and intentionally apply this Identity to your life.

I am Confident Screensaver

Chapter Five

I Am a Conqueror

*No,
in all these things
we are more than conquerors
through him who loved us.*

Romans 8:37

Our two boys are now grown and living on their own. One is happily married while the other is continuing his education at a local university. My wife and I are now raising ten chickens, four cats, and a new puppy. Life is good out on the farm.

Looking back on our family, it's been more than 15 years since my wife and I have had little kids at our table screaming for more chicken nuggets, or more of those little fish crackers—that somehow taste like cheese.

Side note: Fish should not taste like cheese.

When my wife and I go out to a restaurant, we occasionally hear kids from three tables over screaming for more of something. We look at each other for a quick glance and then grin ever so slightly because we fully understand what that mom and dad are going through. "We want more..." is the typical cry every child would announce to all the patrons of the restaurant, hoping the parents will give in one more time for another sweet morsel.

If I didn't have to watch my weight, I'd be eating more of the pickle wraps my mother-in-law always brings to our family events. She knows she cannot show up without these delicious little treats, or there could be trouble.

Just like the little ones at the restaurant three tables over, as adults, we tend to focus more on what we want instead of what we need. We want more cars, boats, fabric in the sewing room, or even more Christmas lights on the house.

I want more.

or

I want to be more.

We may experience the daily barrage of thoughts that clamor for our attention, "I want to be certified or licensed in a particular area." Or, "I'm on a trajectory to have the corner office with the window by a certain age." Let's not forget the title, prestige, and salary that go with that.

Sometimes, I disguise my "I want more" statements with "It would sure be nice to have..." Or, "You know, I don't really need that, but it sure would be nice to see it in my front yard."

Do you ever make those statements?

I would be curious to know what your "more" statements might be. What would you like more of?

More rest?

More solitude?

More money?

More freedom to do what you want?

More can be nice but often it's just not practical or realistic.

We often crave more—whether it's food, rest, or success. But what if 'more' isn't just about what we want, but about who we are? The Bible tells us we are not just conquerors but *more than conquerors*.

*"More than conquerors..." w*hat does that mean to you?

For me, a conqueror is the ultimate hero who operates out of integrity and respect. They are the champion over any foe that might come their way. When all the odds are against them, they still get up and fight no matter how tough the battle is.

I have several friends in my life that I consider to be conquerors. Every day they wake up, get dressed, grab a cup of coffee, and head out the front door just to grind through another new day. Despite the 9 to 5 routine they have mastered over the years, they are internally dealing with hurts, trauma, and abuse of some kind that has affected them even into their adult lives.

However, they keep getting up.

Again, and again.

They look up to the heavens instead of down in defeat. These men are my Friends, my Brothers in Christ, and Warriors on the Battlefield with me.

They are conquerors.

CONQUERORS

In my research, I have looked up 32 different translations of this verse, Romans 8:37, and found that 21 of these translations use the phrase, "more than conquerors..." while other translations use phrases such as "...overwhelming victory...", "...we are more than victorious...", and "...we are triumphantly victorious..."[1]

I like every one of those, and all of them in some way align with a very simplistic Greek definition which is,

to be more than a conqueror[2]

However, like many Greek words, this one has two additional sub-definitions that provide a deeper understanding. Here are their definitions,

to extend benefit (help) that reaches beyond the present situation[3]

and

to prevail[4]

but yet, there is more.

These two definitions above are an off-shoot of this original root definition,

a particular expression of victory, resulting from receiving (obeying) the faith Christ imparts.[5]

If we summed it all up, we might come up with something like the following:

To be *more than a conqueror* means to reach beyond the present situation you are in and to prevail, gain victory, which is a direct result of obeying Christ through the faith imparted to you as a believer.

The identity of "I am a Conqueror" calls us to action—it implies that something is being conquered, that movement is happening.

The identity of I am a Conqueror is a verb that means some type of action is being played out. To be a conqueror means you must be in the act of conquering or have conquered something, right?

But, being a conqueror takes faith and faith is another action word. In his podcast entitled Walking Lessons For Christians Who Sometimes Fall Down, Nate Larkin makes the following statement about faith:

"Faith is more than an intellectual thing. It's there to push us to get off the sofa and go for a walk."[6]

Paul, the writer of Romans clearly defines what we are up against each day as we get out of bed. In verse 35 of chapter 8, we read about the following things that <u>cannot</u> separate us from the love of Christ:

"...trouble or distress or persecution or famine or nakedness or danger or sword..."

Yet, for many of us, as soon as the alarm clock wakes us up with that annoying ring tone we have become so accustomed to, the old tapes start in right away and we begin to focus on all of those things Paul just told us will not separate us from Christ.

It is early in the morning and our day is already out of focus.

Those things mentioned above cannot separate us from Christ because upon accepting Jesus Christ as our Lord and Savior we were immediately set apart for God's glory, for His purpose. The Holy Spirit lives in us — guiding, comforting, and advocating before the Father.

Back on April 17, 1989, I wrote this in my Bible on the introduction page for the book of James...

"Faith is not a defense plan against Satan. It is an attack weapon that allows us to win the battle."

Romans 8:37, is the key to reclaiming your identity as the conqueror God called you to be.

Being in a relationship with Christ does not mean you will not experience any of those things mentioned in verse 35, but it does guarantee you God already knew about the battle, and Christ, through the Holy Spirit is right there in the middle of it with you.

Now that is a promise I can live with. How about you?

In verse 36, Paul makes a statement most of us do not want to hear, or even accept.

"For your sake we face death all day long."

Okay, that does not fit into the fantasy world I can sometimes go to where everything is absolutely perfect. Problems do not exist in that world and there is definitely no talk of facing death.

As Paul continues in verse 37, I can almost imagine him pounding his fist on the podium, passionately declaring as loud as he can, positioning the attention of everyone in listening range...

"No, in all these things we are more than conquerors through Him who loved us."

Paul is declaring to those in the church in Rome that they are already more than a conqueror over any of the items listed in verse 35. Yet, he does not stop there. In verses 38 and 39 he presents them with another list that is more intense than the first.

"For I am convinced that neither death nor life, neither angels nor principalities, neither the present nor the future, nor any powers, neither height nor depth, nor anything else in all creation, will be able to separate us from the love of God that is in Christ Jesus our Lord."

It's important to note we will be challenged by some of these things in our daily lives. Satan will try using any one of the items listed in this last verse to put a wedge between us and our Savior. Some of the items on this list will be things we may experience here on earth while for other items on the list we may need to wait until that glorious day we see Christ face to face.

BELIEVERS ARE SUPER-CONQUERORS[7]

For the longest time this verse has tricked me.

It wasn't until I sat down at my computer one particular morning, at 4:30 am to start writing this chapter that I noticed something I had not paid any attention to before. As I reread Romans 8:37 I realized there is one word in this verse takes the concept of being a conqueror to a whole other level.

You have already read about it a few pages back so feel free to do as I did and re-read the verse again.

Basically, after reading this verse multiple times, I always came up with the same conclusion, I am just a conqueror.

That's it.

Plain and simple.

Period.

There is no more to discuss.

Right?

Wrong.

The difficulty of focusing on just one word is that we can easily miss the greater picture. In this case, the Greek does not provide a stand-alone definition for the word *conqueror*. When you read the Greek definitions earlier, did you notice there was no definition for the word *conqueror*? To get the full meaning of this powerful word, we had to expand it to the phrase "...*we are **more than** conquerors.*" These two simple words allow us to learn about a whole new perspective for this particular identity.

We have already gone to great lengths to explain the word *conqueror* in this verse, but now we need to recognize what I think are two very important keywords, "...*more than*..." Adding the words *more than* in front of *conquerors* means we can now add a cape to our spiritual superhero suit.

I think of David from the Old Testament as *more than a conqueror*. He was selected out of six brothers to become king of Israel at the age of 15. However, before he could take his place on the throne, he had to conquer some enemies of his own. Before he conquered Goliath in front of vast armies, he defeated a lion and a bear single-handedly in the wilderness as they tried to take one of his sheep.

David internally knew he was *more than* a conqueror. As David picked up those five smooth stones, the mocking Philistines might have seemed overwhelming. Goliath's height alone could have cast a shadow over him. But David, standing there, didn't see a giant—he saw another opponent in a long line of trials that had already been defeated

God used sheep, a lion, and a bear to teach David that he was prepared to face a giant.

The question now becomes, how do we become more than conquerors, a Super-Conqueror, as believers in Christ? Part of the equation is looking to our past and noticing the victories God has walked us through. Even if you find the smallest of victories, it is still a victory. The second part of the equation is believing every word that Paul wrote in verse 31,

"What, then, shall we say in response to these things? If God is for us, who can be against us?"

It is impossible to face all of the things in those two lists we looked at on our own. Without Christ in our lives, we would easily succumb to the slightest problem crumbling to the ground in a heap of defeat.

Because of what Christ did on the cross for us, that is the only way we become *more than a conqueror*. In verse 34, Paul writes "Christ Jesus who died... who was raised from death to life—is at the right hand of God and is also interceding for us." In this short sentence, we find four of the most powerful statements that could have ever been written about Christ.

Christ Jesus died – for us on the cross

He was raised from the dead – three days later

He is currently sitting at the right hand of God – His rightful place next to God

He is interceding (praying) for us

Knowing these four truths should for the foundation of our relationship with Christ. We should be able to take a look at any list put before us and declare from the highest of mountaintops or the valleys, we are more than a conqueror. We can be *more than*—when we put our faith in Christ and focus on what can be done through him instead of circumstances that distract us further away from Christ.

"Believers are protected by Christ's crucifixion, resurrection, exaltation, and intercession."[8]

What if the *"more than"* portion of this verse meant that each new day as we put our feet on the floor when getting out of bed, we remember how God gave us the faith to walk through the prior day and declare, I am *more than a conqueror* today than what I was yesterday. Yesterday, through Christ, I conquered a lion and a bear and today, I will conquer a Goliath.

What if every day you woke up knowing you were already victorious? That through Christ, you're not just surviving—you're conquering. What battles would you face differently today?

POINTS TO PONDER

It is a fact that we will face hardships in our lives. However, it is only because of the love of our Heavenly Father, and his son, Jesus Christ, and the Holy Spirit that lives in us, that we can navigate through these difficult times and stand strong as *"more than a conqueror."*

What is your definition of Conqueror?

Now that you have gained a better understanding of the phrase *more than a conqueror*, would you change your definition? What would you change it to and why?

David had private experiences in the wilderness protecting his sheep from a lion and a bear. There was respect for life (protecting the sheep) and an integrity of doing what was right. That is what allowed David to stand before Goliath in front of two armies that were mocking him. Can you reflect back on your life and see when God helped you privately stand your ground?

We learned that to be a conqueror we need faith from God. Look up Hebrews 11:1 and James 1:3 and write out in your own words what faith is and what it produces.

What does Revelation 3:21 tell us about the rewards of being a conqueror?

Write down a few action steps that will allow you to purposefully and intentionally apply this Identity to your life.

I am a Conqueror Screensaver

Chapter Six

I Can Do All Things

I can do all things through him who gives me strength.

Philippians 4:13

Have you ever had the thought, 'I just don't have enough _____ to get through life, (you fill in the blank)?' This is not so much about the material things, but rather the mental and emotional strength to do something.

Some days we are pushed to our limits and find ourselves at a breaking point where we are mentally, physically, and possibly spiritually exhausted. It might be for a day, week, or month when you can't seem to find your way out of the season of being pushed down to the lowest part of your life.

My good friend Eze refers to this "pushed to our limits" status as "living life with the blender on high and the lid off."

What a great description.

I get it because I've been there.

There was a season where I was stuck in the never-ending loop of exhaustion, confusion, and a lack of interest for life. It was one of the worst experiences I have ever gone through. For several years I was in and out of hospitals and counseling offices all due to deep-rooted fear and unresolved anger. I lost jobs because of the mental and physical state I was in and my family suffered greatly.

One job gave me the ultimatum that if I felt like I needed to stay home, regardless of the reason, I needed to call my manager by a certain time in the morning to let him know I could not make it. The physical and mental exhaustion was too great one particular day and I missed a call. That day sealed my fate with the company I worked for and I lost my job. Then, somehow, I was hired as an Assistant General Manager for a nationwide chain store not far from our home. I was working ten-hour days and once again I was mentally and physically pushed to my limits. When re-stocking the shelves I had a major anxiety attack. It was embarrassing enough on its own, but having one in front of co-workers and customers alike, words cannot express the shame and guilt I felt. The General Manager had to help me to a private room where he proceeded to call my wife and ask her to come get me. On that day, I lost my job once again.

Here is a side note about these two companies. They did nothing wrong. In fact, they did everything possible to work with me to have a successful day yet in the long run that blender was spinning way too fast and I did not know how to push the right buttons to make it slow down.

Christ was working through my wife giving her strength as she began managing our household, including two little boys, school activities, finances, her job, and my debilitating mental state was taking a toll on her as well. I knew that Christ was strong, but I have to tell you that my wife comes in a strong second.

During those times, there was no way I could say, "I can do all things…" because I was struggling just to get out of bed to have a cup of coffee before going back to bed for the rest of the day.

There were more times than not that I did not believe in myself, or more importantly, believe what Christ said about me. My Heavenly Father was constantly using my wife as a living testimony of mercy, grace, and love to let me know everything was going to be okay.

Have you ever been in a situation like what I just described; have you been swept down into the all-encompassing death spiral of emotions? That is what I call it. I know it sounds a bit dramatic but it is an effective way to identify the cycle that can quickly get out of control pertaining to our feelings.

Here is an example of an emotional death spiral: shame morphs into fear, spins into guilt, which cascades into embarrassment then loneliness and isolation. How about feeling like a failure and thinking everyone is looking at you? The thoughts you create in your head become a new death spiral because now a new expectation is being formed from what we think other people think of us. In the end, the only thing we want to do is crawl to the darkest corner of the room, grab a blanket, and maybe our favorite stuffed animal, and just become invisible.

That is what I experienced for several years.

I was a failure as a father to my two incredible sons. There was no way I could proudly call myself a husband. I could not even mow the lawn or take out the trash. Holding down a job was impossible, so, as a provider for my family, I failed miserably,

Fear and anger stripped me of my sense of identity. I was lost, confused, and alone. But God wasn't done with me yet. Transformation didn't happen overnight, but step by step, He led me toward healing. So how did I move from a place of despair to confidently declaring, 'I can do all things through Christ'?

Change

How did I go from a broken, on-my-knees man who literally could not do anything to someone who is standing tall and confident because of who I am in Christ? How is it that now I can, with great enthusiasm, declare, "I <u>can</u> do all things through Him (Christ) that strengthens me."

What made the change?

Shifting from 'I can't' to 'I can' wasn't easy. There was no magic moment—no Broadway-style musical where I woke up singing my worries away. As a matter of fact, I'm still learning to lean into Christ even more each new day He gives me.

It is a journey and a process.

It is one day at a time.

I started by doing one thing, stopping, taking a deep breath, and then adding one more thing. It was slow, tedious, and even draining, but I did it, and I am still doing it.

"Every small step toward your goals matters because progress, no matter how small, is still progress."[1]

It is the small steps we take every day that allow us to change from "I can't" to "I can."

Here are some of the things I began to do.

Three-Legged Stool

Three-legged stools are great, and they have three legs for a reason. If you take one leg away from the stool, what happens? You become unbalanced and you are likely to tip over. What if, you take two legs away, then what happens? When sitting on what you thought was a firm flat surface, means you'll end up on the floor because the last leg of the stool has no way of supporting you. Knowing it was time to leave the dark corner of depression behind, I intentionally created my own foundational mental, physical, and spiritual three-legged stool.

I had to come up with something more motivational than the fear and anger that plagued me on a daily basis. My three-legged stool had to have a tangible aspect so I could see the results of my efforts. Here is an example of how I labeled each leg of the three-legged stool.

Leg one: M*y **relationship with God*** is more important than the reasons for my fear and anger.

Leg two: M*y **relationship with my wife, sons, and extended family*** is more important than the reasons for my fear and anger.

Leg three: M*y **relationship with myself*** is more important than the reasons for my fear and anger.

With these labels in place, I added three bullet points under each title describing why that specific leg was so important. Lastly, I found a Bible verse to support the individual groupings. This was all written down in my journal.

JOURNALING

Now there's a word that can strike fear into the hearts of any man and some women. Many men don't like sitting down for any amount of time to write down their thoughts. Men are "doers" and "fixers." Let's be honest—some of us need a codebreaker to read our handwriting. Ladies on the other hand are more likely to journal. The pages of their journal might have those cute call-out bubbles, and flowers and butterflies in the margins. They might even use three or four colored pens to organize their thoughts.

Up until three years ago, I did not even like the word journaling let alone the thought of actually writing in a book with just a bunch of lines. Here are a few benefits I have received from taking the time to write something down in an empty book.

- Write down a problem and then find scripture that teaches me biblical principles for growth in Christ.

- Studying parts of the Bible, listing out my Observations, Interpretation, and Application.

- Writing in my journal helps clear my mind of jumbled thoughts, which significantly reduces the worry and anxiety.

- Looking back through the pages of my journal, I can visually re-visit what I've learned, which reinforces my growth in Christ.

In my journal, I write down what kind of day I am having, what I am feeling, and why. I also write out my devotions, one verse at a time. What was once considered to be an egregious attack on my time has now become something of great importance.

Give it a try; you might find it helpful.

CONNECTION

Fear, anger, guilt, and shame, along with so many other feelings push us to a disconnected life. That death spiral continues to spin out of control and we isolate ourselves from the most important people in our lives, our friends and families, and even our relationship with our Savior.

Somehow the ever-changing moods we fall into warp our sense of feeling making us think we can handle life on our own. "I don't need anybody. Besides, I already know what they think about me. Life is better on my own."

"Disconnection leads to dislocation, dysfunction, death – What is not connected will not grow."[2]

Men dig their heels in and believe the mental lie, "I am a man, and I can deal with this. I don't need any help." If you are a woman, you might think, "I have to stand up tall and confident, manage the house, the kids, my husband, my job, volunteering at the food bank, church, or school. I can do it all because everyone's expectation is telling me I am supposed to be a superwoman."

When we isolate ourselves, we create the perfect environment for the devilish death spiral to put cracks in our foundation. Eventually, those cracks become deeper and deeper and we are left crumbling to utter despair. The legs of our stool are being ripped out from under us.

"The thief comes only to steal and kill and destroy..." John 10:10

GOD'S WORD

God had been trying to stay in a relationship with me even though for years there was no reciprocation on my part. For far too long I had believed what fear and anger told me about myself and I avoided reading even a single verse, so my Bible stayed where I put it, quietly on the bookshelf collecting dust. Eventually, through the prompting of the Holy Spirit, a small idea began to grow in my heart. Find your Bible and start reading it.

This is the most important must-have step that I implemented into my daily life. It was time for me to run back into the arms of my Heavenly Father. I needed his love, comfort, peace, and forgiveness.

For those who might argue they can do a better job of navigating through life on their own, please note the following. Nowhere in the Bible does it say we are to face difficulties on our own, instead, its pages are filled with examples of others coming alongside someone else to help.

Aaron and Hur held up Moses's arms.

Ruth was loyal to Naomi.

Paul and Barnabas worked together to spread the gospel.

Jonathan and David had a friendship unlike any other.

Paul had several brothers in Christ at his side on various missionary trips and who even visited him while he was in prison.

Christ had 70 disciples, with twelve of them being in His inner circle, and Peter, James, and John even closer.

It can be tough inviting others into our lives, or to be accepted into the lives of others, but we must pursue this connection at all costs. Being vulnerable before Christ helps us to be transparent before others. Sharing our struggles with others can create lasting friendships, supportive prayer, and a Christ-like love beyond measure.

"I can..." – is the beginning.

"...do all things..." – is the continuation.

"...through Christ..." – is the source.

"...who gives me strength." – is the power

"This reflects the Christian belief that it is not by human effort alone that one achieves strength, but through a relationship with Jesus Christ. It is only through Christ's life, death, and resurrection that believers are empowered to face life's challenges. This divine empowerment is not a one-time event but an ongoing process. It is a continuous action on Christ's part to his followers."[3]

Within this relationship, Christ is the one ... *who gives me (us) strength.* (emphasis added)

When reading 2 Corinthians 12:7-10, Paul confesses he struggled with some type of problem, to the point of calling God to his side for help. The intensity and focus Paul had was more than profound and serves as an example that even in really difficult moments, believers in Christ can utter ever so silently the same words of intentionality as listed below.

"...to keep me from becoming conceited..." – the outward problem

"...I was given a thorn in my flesh..." – a gift to identify the inward problem

"...three times I pleaded with the Lord..." – acknowledging just how weak he was

"...My grace is sufficient for you..." – Christ's healing through the relationship

"...for my power is made perfect in weakness..." – Christ's ongoing strength

Here's a thought worth considering about Paul's confession. Imagine if he identified what the "thorn in the flesh" was. With that one admission, he could have changed the whole trajectory of the New Testament and how believers in Christ rely on God's grace. Hypothetically, let's say Paul struggled with eating an overabundance of M&M's. The problem was so bad that he could not stop, no matter what he tried. If Paul shared the problem he had, then throughout the centuries, believers would have only focused on that one thing Paul struggled with—an uncontrollable compulsion for something as trivial as candy-coated chocolate. The argument would have shifted from "God's power was made perfect in Paul's weakness" to "God's power is made perfect in only one specific weakness, eating too many M&M's. Okay, the M&M's example might be a stretch but it still conveys the overall purpose in Paul's vagueness which allows readers from every walk of life to identify with it in some fashion.

It may be hard for some of us to understand, but Paul eventually turned the difficulties of the "thorn in the flesh" into a gift from God. A question that comes to mind is, as believers in Christ, are we able to acknowledge the weaknesses, insults, hardships, persecutions, and difficulties as Paul did and accept the plan God has for us? Can we walk with the same strength he was able to do?

"When (we) are weak the Lord is strong and demonstrates His strength through us – *this empowerment enables them to endure trials, perform their duties, and live out their faith effectively.*"[4]

Honestly, when I'm really tired and haven't had my cup of coffee yet, it becomes very easy to let the thoughts run rampant. Instead of staying strong like Paul, I can turn inward and be the only participant in an over-the-top pity party. Sometimes, if I'm not careful, one small thought can snowball into a full-blown mental storm for me. I can start ruminating on thoughts which can then escalate into a really huge brain-storm. But, like Paul, I must, we must take every thought captive, making it obedient to Christ. When I take my eyes off of myself and put them on Christ, my attitude and behavior change from

I can't...

to

I can.

We don't feel our way into the strength of Christ—we believe our way into it. When we shift our focus from self-doubt to Christ's power, we move from 'I can't' to 'I can.' This isn't just motivation—it's a reality. In Him, we are empowered to do all things

POINTS TO PONDER

When the death spiral hits we get caught up in the chaos, feeling there is no way out. Hitting the pause button on the blender is just not happening. Our brains have become wired to give in and say "I can't."

"Your nervous system will always choose familiar chaos over unfamiliar peace until you learn to heal and choose differently."[5]

Taking one small step forward each day is an actionable way of saying, "I can..." The benefit we have as believers is that Christ has given us the Holy Spirit, who reminds us that the strength we need comes from Christ's sacrifice on the cross.

If you decide to create your own motivational three-legged stool, build it so that if one leg is neglected then the whole stool and your way of life are affected—and you notice it. Spend the badly needed time on this part of your "I can" statement. This is not a race to see who finishes the quiz first. This is your life and your life is important. Be intentional and purposeful.

Are you currently going through an "I can't" season? If so, take a moment to identify the reasons behind the feelings of "I can't." What are the messages coming from the death spiral or blender on high effect?

The Bible has several examples of how God's people were in difficult situations and He turned the "I can't" into the "I can". What did it look like when you recognized the nudge the Holy Spirit was giving you? What changed and how did it make an impact in your life?

If you are walking in an "I can" type of relationship with Christ right now, describe your belief system and how that is working better than the death spiral of random and chaotic feelings.

As a believer in Christ, you can confidently know that He is constantly giving you the strength needed to put your feet on the floor again and stand, write down a few ways you can apply this verse, Philippians 4;13 to your life today.

Write down a few action steps that will allow you to purposefully and intentionally apply this Identity to your life.

I Can Do All Things Screensaver

Chapter Seven

I AM FEARLESS

*For the Spirit God gave us
does not make us timid,
but gives us power,
love and self-discipline.*

2 Timothy 1:7

What is the first thing that comes to mind when you see the word fearless?

Quickly, now.
Do not think about all the peripheral pieces to it.
Focus on this one word, fearless.
What does it mean for you?
Hold on to that thought.
That feeling.
Does it trigger certain memories or feelings?
Where in your past does it take you?
Where in the future would you like it to take you?
What definition would you give to fearless?
What example would you provide?

Take a moment and write down your answers to the corresponding questions in your journal.

BACK STORY

This was the final time Paul the Apostle would be imprisoned—and the last letter he ever wrote. This time, though, would be different. No more guards to watch over him day and night. No more angels or earthquakes breaking open the cell doors. No more reunions with fellow believers.

The Roman authorities had had enough of this New Testament preacher and had an end plan in mind. Historians say that at the time 2nd Timothy was being written, Paul was in a cistern-type dungeon twelve feet below ground. Roman citizens were not allowed to be fed to the lions by law, so instead, they were thrown into a cold, dark, holding cell, waiting for the authorities to decide their fate.

In his second letter to Timothy, Paul acknowledged to his friend that his time was drawing near, and Emperor Nero would ensure that this Christ influencer might be silenced once and for all.

For me, this is where things would get difficult. If I were in Paul's situation my mind would be racing, trying to figure out how to control the next step. I would be overwhelmed by the situation and filled with anxiety, feeding the ever-increasing fear that was turning into an uncontrollable monster. Remember, the prisoners in these cells never saw the light of day again.

I am extremely thankful that God chose Paul to be Paul and me to be me. I do not know if I could have endured everything he did. He was Fearless. He Feared Less.

While Paul was imprisoned and living out his last days, I wonder if he felt an urgency to pen this letter to Timothy, who was facing his own set of difficulties. As a young man, Timothy was already commissioned to be the pastor of the church in Ephesus. This was no small task since the church was dealing with diverse cultures and false teachings. As Paul was in the most deplorable situation possible, he was writing his friend a letter of encouragement and guidance.

This attitude—this behavior of Paul's—is indicative of what he wrote in Romans 8:37-39.

> *"No, in all these things we are more than conquerors through him who loved us. For I am convinced that neither death nor life, neither angels nor demons, neither the present nor the future, nor any powers, neither height nor depth, nor anything else in all creation, will be able to separate us from the love of God that is in Christ Jesus our Lord."*

As Paul's life was coming to an end, the baton was being passed to Timothy. Step up to the plate. Be confident. Be strong. This is not the time to shy away from your calling. Wavering in your faith or responsibilities is not even a question to be asked.

Paul used the Greek word, *deilia* (di-lee'-ah), which is only mentioned once in the New Testament, and it means,

> *timidity, cowardice, fearfulness. This is often contrasted with the boldness and courage that comes from faith in God. It describes a lack of confidence that hinders one's ability to act in faith and obedience.*[1]

I can understand some of what Timothy might have been going through. There was a time in my life when things were going really well. My relationship with Christ was spot on and I was involved in various church ministries. One evening at church, I had the immense privilege of sharing my testimony in front of a packed house. It received a positive response by 99.5% of those in attendance. However, I let the .5% ruin the night for me.

After the service, a few people approached me and said some hurtful things as they disagreed with the redemptive work Christ had done in my heart and life. Even though I knew in my heart they were the ones who were really hurting, I took those statements and unfortunately chose to make them personal. Because of the statements those individuals said, I did what I had learned to do at a very early age and I withdrew allowing the sting of their words to go straight to my heart. Over the years I was reluctant to be *fearless* because I had been living as a coward for far too long.

Paul's fearlessness was unwavering, even as he faced death. Timothy was called into leadership in a difficult time, and he couldn't afford to let fear hold him back. But what about us? I struggled with this newfound fear for quite a long time, and I'm still learning to walk in a fearless relationship with Christ. How would you respond when fear whispers that you're not enough?

Here are some examples of friends of mine being fearless at different times of their lives.

NEEDING HELP

When I first began organizing my thoughts for this chapter, I struggled with how to approach this fierce topic. After praying about what to do, I believe God gave me a great idea and it would involve my friends.

I contacted our small group leader and asked if I could have a few minutes during our next meeting to ask everyone's opinion about being *fearless*. Those few minutes turned into about an hour as we all shared our personal fearless stories.

When my wife and I arrived at the Rich's home, everyone was already at the large family dining room table that seats 10 people comfortably. We were the last to show up and thankfully, our group of friends had left some snacks for us to enjoy.

The directions that night were rather simple; write down your definition of the word *fearless* and then provide an example of what fearless looks like to you. Once everyone was done, they asked me to read them out loud to see if we could figure out who wrote them. We had a great time discussing each of our answers.

It was amazing to read nine different definitions and examples of being fearless.[2]

Here are a few of them.

"To be unafraid; totally confident in my ability to persevere, overcome doubt and fear."

"Facing a diagnosis of Chronic Lymphocytic Leukemia and living with a fungal infection and prostate cancer. I am totally okay right now with care providers and whatever the future holds."

One of the veterans in our group, who served on the U.S.S. Midway took time to disclose a definition just as meaningful.

"To accomplish a task that is physically dangerous, that must be done, to the point of death, but doing that task anyway."

Here's the example he gave...

"[I] volunteered to suit up to fight a shipboard fire (on the U.S.S. Midway) after an explosion that decimated our at-sea fire party. They were investigating a report of smoke in a starboard compartment below decks. I did a lot of praying subconsciously."

One of the other men in the group, who is usually a very quiet guy, wrote something down that we all should have taken notice of. Here are his thoughts.

"Without fear."

"I don't fear death, because Jesus died for me, and because of that, the next place I go will be a lot better."

Two of the ladies in our group who are like two peas in a pod if you ask me, both gave very similar responses to our exercise.

One wrote...

"Unafraid to move into the unknown"

"Speaking to someone I don't know wondering if they will receive me in a positive [way], but I speak to them anyway – ready to get any kind of response – positive or negative."

While the other penned the following...

"Bravery – not afraid to do, say, or behave in a way that would have any type of consequence. Confidence that you could handle the outcome of being fearless."

Her example was...

"Speaking truth in a situation that isn't popular to what society wants, or accepted. Standing up for our faith."

When all of the world is looking at us and throwing their perceptions of who they think we should be, demanding we conform to their ideals, Paul wrote to Timothy, to us, saying

"...God [has given] us a spirit of power, love, and self-control." (emphasis added)

WHO?

The question begs to be asked, "If the worldly standards we are so accustomed to don't work, then where do we go for help? Who helps us out with becoming *fearless*?"

Paul addresses this question within the first two words of this verse, *"For God..."*

The world spews out unsustainable ideas of how to cope with power, love, and self-control, as defined by its standards, but Paul takes us back to the core of where these gifts originally come from: God.

"His divine power has given us everything we need for a godly life through our knowledge of him who called us by his own glory and goodness." 2 Peter 1:3

"And hope does not put us to shame, because God's love has been poured out into our hearts through the Holy Spirit, who has been given to us." Romans 5:5

"For the grace of God has appeared that offers salvation to all people. It teaches us to say 'No' to ungodliness and worldly passions, and to live self-controlled, upright and Godly lives in this present age." Titus 2:11-12

Different authors of the bible, throughout hundreds of years, recognized that the *Lord **is*** the source of the power, love, and self-control mentioned in 2 Timothy 1:7.

Let's shift gears and look at the kind of power Paul wanted Timothy—and us—to truly understand.

LET'S BLOW SOMETHING UP

Hollywood has perfected the act of blowing things up. It seems a movie isn't a movie unless there are explosions ignited by a stick of dynamite. When Timothy was facing the difficulties within the church, he may have felt like some type of Hollywood bombs were going off as he dealt with the various types of division within the church. However, Paul is sharing with this young Pastor the power that comes from the Holy Spirit is a power unlike anything Hollywood could produce.

The problems infiltrating the church in Ephesus were the cause of great concern for Timothy. Paul needed to remind this timid preacher that God is the source of the power and strength needed to withstand the problems in the church he is leading. The power Paul describes doesn't go boom—it goes "WOW"—and it differs greatly from the destructive red stick that Hollywood uses.

The power described here is defined as *"for the believer, power to achieve by applying the Lord's inherent abilities. 'Power through God's ability.'"*[3]

This definition comes from the Greek word *dunamis* which is where we get the word dynamite. Imagine what this might look like for a believer in Christ. We fully understand the physical effects of what a stick of dynamite can do but do we fully grasp the *dunamis* that has been given to each of us as believers in Christ?

This *power*, that Paul is encouraging Timothy with is the same power that raised Christ from the dead.

"I pray that the eyes of your heart may be enlightened in order that you may know the hope..., and his incomparably great power for us who believe. That power is the same as the mighty strength he exerted when he raised Christ from the dead..."[4]

This is the power that allows us to fight during a Chronic Lymphocytic Leukemia diagnosis, or, voluntarily suiting up to fight a shipboard fire after an explosion that decimated the at-sea fire party. When we are overwhelmed with trauma, abuse, or chaos, this *power* from God is what allows us to stand, just like Timothy, to face another day.

I do not have the capability of understanding what it means to sacrificially give my life up for someone, especially if I do not know them. Somehow, I think it might be easier for me to comprehend there are galaxies billions of light years away from us with millions of planets and stars in each one than fully grasping the type of love God, through Christ, has for me, for us.

If we removed all the verses from the Bible and left only one, I would like to think the most important verse left would be John 3:16.

"For God so loved the world that he gave his one and only Son, that whoever believes in him shall not perish but have eternal life."

The two-fold message here is Christ's sacrificial love for us should be the motivating factor that drives us to love others.

LOVE, LOVE, LOVE

When we run into the arms of our Savior we learn "There is no fear in love. But perfect love drives out fear..."[5] Within this relationship we understand there is a perfect love and while in the presence of this perfect love fear cannot exist. For me, fear equals judgment and rejection but as I daily walk with Christ I experience acceptance and confidence.

There have been occasions when life was really tough and the old tapes of what I learned as a young boy quietly began to play in the background of my thoughts. These tapes would constantly remind me that I was alone, worthless, and not important. Fear plagued me on a daily basis keeping me a prisoner chained up in a forgotten dark and dank cell. Like Timothy, I had to find the courage to face these difficulties head on through the spirit of power, love, and self-control.

When I began to change my way of thinking from an inward, self pity, *woe-is-me* mentality to reaching out to others helping them to break the weighted chains around their wrists and ankles. The fear that once held me captive had to leave. I realized that fear cannot be in the same room as the love of Christ. The more we fearlessly love others the more we are set free from the bondage of fear itself.

Paul is encouraging a very young Timothy to be an example of this sacrificial love for others, especially in a new church that is being infiltrated with false teachings, persecution, and infighting. Paul was trying to help his friend understand this spirit of love was not just a warm soft cuddly feeling but an active force of God's nature that dispels all fear.

DISCIPLINE

I would like to think that I am really good at being disciplined, especially in those areas I have experience in. Yet, I struggle with having discipline in the new things I'm beginning to learn. Learning is supposed to be fun and educating—not intimidating and scary, right? Another problem is that I can easily justify scrolling through social media longer than I should or filling my plate with more food than my doctor recommends. Two games on my phone only take up a short amount of time—ahh, not really. They take up a lot of time. Those are ways of NOT being disciplined.

Have you ever felt that way?

I am learning, however, that being disciplined in the easy things can lead to a greater sense of accomplishment and confidence which in turn encourages me to try something else that is new. Seeing the results of this confidence, I have noticed I become fearless—because I am fearless.

Paul finishes this verse of admonishment for Timothy by emphasizing the importance of *self-control* which is mentioned only this one time in the New Testament.

"This term emphasizes the importance of inner restraint and the ability to govern one's desires and impulses in accordance with godly wisdom."[6]

There it is: inner strength and the ability to govern one's desires and impulses.

When I am well-rested and able to be fully present in the situation, I would like to think I am better at managing my desires and impulses. When I am tired and without coffee, watch out because my responses turn into reactions. Once again, I can easily justify my behavior for getting grumpy. "I'm too old to learn anything new. This is just the way I am. It's how I've always done things, and no one's going to tell me to do it differently."

As a young inexperienced pastor of a large church, Timothy could have just as easily dealt with those in his flock shouting out the same excuses. After a while, he had to have been discouraged and worn down. As a timid minister, I can only imagine the struggles he faced. "I'm supposed to be the leader of this church and I'm afraid to step up and take control. What if they don't like me? God, I know you have called me to do this, but…"

Here are two thoughts to consider about our reactions and Timothy's apprehension. First, telling someone "I'm too old to change, besides, this is just the way I am" is a complete cop-out. That is a worldly excuse for giving yourself permission to act however you want which selfishly says you know what is better for your life than God. That is a scary road to travel on. Secondly, when looking back at both the definition of *self-control* and the 2 Timothy 1:7 verse we find the source of strength behind our self-control, *"…godly wisdom,"* and *"…God [has given us] self-control."* (emphasis added)

When we react to a situation that means we are pushing God out of the picture and saying "I know what's best." When we stop, breathe, and slow down we respond according to the divine nature God has directly imparted to each one of us. Paul urged Timothy to do the same, pause, breathe, and think about how Christ would want you to respond.

Fear Less

The identity "I am Fearless" is the opposite of "…a spirit of timidity…" and that is mainly what we have focused on in this chapter. However, when we purposefully walk in the spirit of power, love, and self-control God has given us we

fear

less.

Many of us are afraid to change because of the difficult journey of healing we would have to embark on. It can feel safer to just stay the way we are. Ignore the pain. Ignore the trauma. Ignore the bullying. Ignore the abuse. But there is hope and healing through what Christ did on the cross.

Remember the quiet guy from my Bible study group? This was his definition of Fearless,

"Without fear."

Can it really be that simple?

He fears less because he is secure in his relationship and identity in Christ. Essentially, Paul is telling Timothy, and all fellow believers to stop worrying, God's got this. Fear doesn't have the final say. Christ does. You are not a slave to fear—you are empowered by His Spirit. Today, step into the power, love, and self-control that is already yours in Christ. You don't have to wait to be fearless. You are fearless. Walk in it.

POINTS TO PONDER

Remember,
   Fear says "You can't"
   Christ says "You can"
   Fear says "Resist the change and stay the same."
   Christ says "You are a new creation."
   Fear says, "You will lose control."
   Christ says, "I've got you."
There are 365 verses in the bible that use the phrase "Fear not!", "Be not afraid!", "Have no fear!", or "Do not be afraid." I would like to think all of those verses culminate with 2 Timothy 1:7 "I am Fearless", what do you think?

Are there one or two things you hide that might need to be brought to the forefront? Better yet, can you create a list of things you are good at but need some self-control in because they take up a lot of time as well?

What is your definition of the word fear?

What is your definition of the word fearless?

What example can you provide from your own life where fear has tried to control you and prevent you from walking in Christ as a Fearless believer?

When we walk in full belief and understanding of who we are in Christ, the problems of this world lose their grip on us. What are some specific situations you are currently going through that you would like to be free of? To walk in freedom from?

Write down three specific ways you will apply this identity, I am Fearless, to the situations you are currently facing.

What are your thoughts about these verses:
Isaiah 41:10

Psalms 3:3

Psalms 118:6

2 Thessalonians 3:3

Psalms 46:10

Write down a few action steps that will allow you to purposefully and intentionally apply this Identity to your life.

I am Fearless Screensaver

Chapter Eight
I Am Forgiven

*In him we have redemption through his blood,
the forgiveness of sins,
in accordance with the riches of God's grace.*

Ephesians 1:7

Forgiveness seems simple—but if you're human, you know it rarely is.

Haven't we all struggled with giving and receiving forgiveness? I'm guessing that most of us have a general understanding of forgiveness, but we may find living in the freedom Christ provides through forgiveness is often much harder. This chapter—and Chapter 15, *I Am Valuable*—are the two most important identities discussed in this book. Even though they are intricately tied together, we need to take the time to understand their importance separately.

We will use the following three questions as guideposts to understanding forgiveness. In each section, we will take the time to figure out why the answers are so important and how to apply what we have learned to our newfound identity, I Am Forgiven.

Question #1 - What does re*demption* mean?

Question #2 - Why do we need *forgiveness*?

Question #3 - How should my forgiven identity influence my interactions with others?

Before we can tackle the huge topic of forgiveness, we need to take the initial steps of understanding why we need redemption and forgiveness in the first place.

SEPARATION

It's been several years since my two sons moved out on their own. Yet, I still remember when they were younger and while living at home, their mother and I found the need to set specific rules that followed this principle: If you do this, then you will get this. If you disobey, then there will be consequences for your actions. If you're a parent, you've probably set similar boundaries for your children. Implementing these rules can be difficult, but without them, the parent-child relationship becomes very disconnected.

Just as our children have parents, believers in Christ have God as our Heavenly Father, and He enjoyed an intimate relationship with Adam and Eve in the Garden of Eden. Like any loving parent, there was only one rule or commandment he wanted them to obey.

"And the LORD God commanded the man, '...you must not eat from the tree of the knowledge of good and evil, for when you eat from it you will certainly die.'" Genesis 2:16-17

At that moment, God established the principle of cause and effect in His relationship with humanity: 'If you do this, then this will happen.'

When Adam and Eve ate fruit from the Tree of Knowledge, they gave in to the serpent's temptation. The serpent's deception became the starting point for Eve's disobedience which then influenced Adam. Satan focused on the idea that God was withholding something good from them and she decided to give in to that lie as mentioned in Genesis 3:5. It's important to note the temptation by itself was not the sin, but it became sin when her heart's desire was acted upon. Then, Eve gave Adam the same fruit, which he willfully ate in disobedience. At that point, sin immediately separated them from God because sin entered the world.

James, the half-brother of Jesus, clearly understood this principle when he wrote

"But each person is tempted when they are dragged away by their own evil desire and enticed. Then, after desire has conceived, it gives birth to sin; and sin, when it is full-grown, gives birth to death." James 1:14-15

Just like any good parent, God realized his children did the exact opposite of what he instructed them to do. With a broken heart, He then dispensed the consequences to His children as listed in Genesis 3:14-21. Like children caught doing something wrong, Adam and Eve shifted the blame to the serpent for causing them to disobey. However, we need to remember God did not give this mandate to the serpent, He gave it to Adam and Eve. They were the ones responsible for obeying, or disobeying, God.

Yes, they were tempted.

Yes, they made a willful decision based upon that temptation.

Yes, they disobeyed God.

Their relationship with God was immediately severed the moment they disobeyed. This act of rebellion became known as 'original sin' and has plagued mankind ever since.

Redemption, through Christ, was God's plan for all of humanity and the only thing that could bring us back into a right relationship with him.

REDEMPTION

As a little boy, I loved throwing rocks into streams, ponds, and lakes. I loved hearing the sound the rock made when hitting the water and seeing the splash that came afterward. One thing I began to notice is that the smaller the rock, the fewer the number of ripples flowing outward from where the rock hit the water. It was the big rocks that made the bigger splashes, and the ripples traveled further across the surface of the water.

I am amazed at the enormity of how one rock, one decision made by Adam and Eve, could affect the whole of humanity. The only way to restore this relationship is to implement a plan of restoration, a plan of redemption, and that brings us to our first question: What does 'redemption' mean?

As we begin to answer this question, learning the definition of *redeemed | redeeming | redeems* is a great place to start. When Paul wrote the book of Ephesians, he used a Greek word for redemption that means,

release affected by payment of ransom[1]

and the Merriam-Webster dictionary provides an exceptional definition as well,

To free from what distresses or harms: such as to free from captivity by payment of ransom, to release from blame or debt.[2]

Here's how I would connect these two definitions of redemption: "Because of an act so harmful and egregious that has held mankind captive, a ransom had to be paid to rescue those held captive."

When I hear the word *redemption*, a thought that comes to mind is about paying off a long-standing bill. Once that last check is written and I know there is a zero balance, a weight is lifted off my shoulders. A ransom, my final payment, has been paid for the debt owed.

Here's an idea to mull over as it pertains to redemption. What about forgiving a debt someone owes you? No strings attached. No conditions. No thought of holding it against them. Just a note showing a zero balance with the red-lettered stamp that declares, "Paid in Full." That's what it means to be redeemed. However, we need to fully understand that the redemption Christ afforded every person is one that money cannot buy and we cannot work for it. Bartering is completely out of the question, and the number of social media likes or comments, followers, or heart emojis won't even come close to securing our redemption in Christ.

Looking back at the definition, we are reminded that redemption means "*by payment of ransom*". The ransom payment for sin was Christ's death on the cross, which is considered a "*gift of God*" according to Ephesians 2:8-9. When Christ said, "*It is finished*" from the cross, John 19:30 He meant that, in that moment, the full weight of every sin, past, present, and future, was put on his shoulders. Jesus bore the weight of our sins. It is because of his shed blood, the sins of all believers in Christ are completely covered. That sacrifice is what allows us back into a relationship with Christ. That is the act that redeems us.

FORGIVENESS

A point to consider is that at the exact moment of our conception, the nature of sin was woven into our DNA. David confesses this fact in Psalm 51:5.

Surely I was sinful at birth, sinful from the time my mother conceived me."

The guilt and weight of this inborn sinful condition separate us from God. Think of it this way, if sin is our inherited condition, then forgiveness is the greatest need we deeply long for. But why is forgiveness so important? What does Scripture reveal about its necessity in reconciling us to a right relationship with God?

Let's first recognize that regardless of our self-diagnosis of whether or not we have sinned, Romans 3:23 is extremely clear on this matter,

"For all have sinned and fall short of the glory of God."

Notice, if you will, there is no delineation of time for when sin has occurred. In other words, Paul doesn't say, "Only those who lived within a particular time in history have sinned." On the contrary, everyone ever born was, has, or will automatically take on a sinful nature because we live in a fallen and sinful world.

The second factor to note is that there is absolutely no identifier of what kind of sin is acceptable and what is not acceptable. Scripture acknowledges that some sins carry greater consequences than others, as seen in John 19:11 and Matthew 11:20-24, however, the bottom line remains the same: all sin separates us from God.

Okay, so we live in a sinful world with a sinful nature, and we've all sinned, now what?

When I was growing up in church, I don't think I paid too much attention to the pastor if he ever preached on forgiveness. It wasn't until my early twenties that I heard an impactful teaching on this subject matter, and I wanted to implement it into my life. The first couple of times I tried forgiving people, it didn't go well. I created certain expectations of how the "forgiveness" conversation should happen between me and the other people, unfortunately, though, they didn't get the memo explaining my expectations, and the discussion went south rather quickly. Even though over time, I feel I have a better understanding of the biblical principle of forgiveness, there is a continued problem of my messing up and the continual need to ask for forgiveness.

Does that sounds familiar?

Christ's sacrificial act of dying on the cross for each of us, pouring out his blood for us, is the only thing that can cover the multitude of sins we need forgiveness for. When accepting Christ as our Savior and asking for His forgiveness, we are immediately and permanently forgiven.

An encouraging way we can walk in forgiveness is to grasp the full intent of 1 John 1:7, which states, *"But if we walk in the light, as he is in the light, we have fellowship with one another, and the blood of Jesus, his Son, purifies us from all sin."*

There was a time in my life when all I could think of were the things I'd done wrong. I'm talking about lying, cheating, and addictive behaviors that led to depression and anxiety. Because of my stupid decisions, I forced people to step up to the plate in ways that never should have happened. I disappointed friends, family members, and incredible co-workers. All these sins, from my standpoint, are things I should never have been forgiven for.

You might be reading this and thinking, "Oh please, the list of things you've done doesn't even compare to what I've done, forgiveness will never happen for me."

I fully understand those statements. They are real, and valuable, and bear witness to what is happening in your heart. Those are familiar statements Christ has heard repeated throughout the centuries from people who have been hurt, traumatized, and abused. These are statements from people who have been abandoned, pushed down, and discarded. Christ accepted all of these hurts and put them on himself so you and I could walk in freedom, joy, and grace. So, we could walk in forgiveness.

Remember, 1 John 1:7 states, *"...the blood of Jesus Christ purifies us from **all** sin."* (emphasis added)

Forgiveness establishes a new and permanent relationship with God through His Son, Jesus Christ. Forgiveness means the debt for our sins has been paid in full.

Once I began to understand the principle of forgiveness afforded me through Christ, I knew I had to start forgiving others as well.

This now becomes a great time to answer Question #3.

FORGIVE THEM

So how should my forgiven identity influence my interactions with others? I feel it's easier to walk away from a cruise ship dessert buffet than tackle this question.

Hurt, anger, and resentment are real, and they run deep when it comes to unforgiveness. We would rather become like a caged lion behind the iron bars at a zoo, pacing back and forth, than forgive someone who has destroyed our innocent world. Trauma and abuse hold the keys to our freedom, and they refuse to relinquish their control. Forgiving those who have hurt us is the last thing on our minds.

The sermons or teachings about forgiveness seem to have no strength or power to help us escape the small and confining cell. We have become judge, prosecutor, and jury toward those who have offended us because we believe it is the only way to gain some semblance of control. We have settled the argument that it is better to live in unforgiveness than run the gauntlet toward freedom. The toll of refusing to forgive others bears down on us, forcing us to an even slower pace as the lion behind iron bars. The longer we refuse to relinquish this control, the sooner we accept defeat as it becomes the new norm. The prison cell is no longer cold, dark, and musty, but instead, it is comfortable, secure, and safe.

Even though that is an extremely dramatic look at the part unforgiveness can play in our lives, once we pull back the curtains, this description holds a lot of truth.

VICTIM -VS- FREEDOM

Everyone deals with hurt and heals from hurt differently. However, in the end, it all comes down to how complicated we make the process of forgiving others.

Unforgiveness demands we stay the victim.

Forgiveness declares we walk in freedom.

Unforgiveness tightens the leg irons around our ankles and prevents us from taking another step toward the open cell door.

Forgiveness gracefully opens the prison doors to a new life where we can walk away from the shackles that once bound us.

When approaching the subject of forgiving someone, it is easy for the defensive walls to go up and allow the pain to rage inside us, trying to claim another day like a rite of passage. We believe the lie that if we mentally hold the other person hostage for just one more day, their day will be ruined, but not ours.

Josh McDowell and Ben Bennett describe how we can get locked into this behavior,

> Even when we understand the truth (of forgiveness), it is difficult to break away from the ingrained thought patterns that influence our behavior... We are similar to the circus elephant whose leg is attached to a stake with a bicycle chain. How can such a flimsy chain restrain such a powerful animal? The creature remains chained because of a memory. The chain was first attached when it was very young, and every effort to pull free proved futile. The elephant learned that the chain was stronger than it was, and it carried this lesson into adulthood. Though strong enough as a full-grown elephant to escape, he is conditioned to captivity. (emphasis added)[3]

Throughout the New Testament, the concept of *forgiveness* is referenced 186 times, carrying with it definitions such as: release, to send away, to grant freely, to forgive.

When Jesus was dying on the cross, one of the last things he uttered was "*Father, forgive them, for they do not know what they are doing.*"[4]

That's what he said, "*Forgive them...*"

It's interesting to note that Jesus never asked to sit down with anyone who had any remote connection to his impending death on the cross and tell them his feelings were hurt and that he did not like what they had done or were going to do to him. When it came to his trial and the grueling walk to Golgotha, not once did he try to defend himself. Not once did he try to convince or sway the crowd's opinion.

"*Father, forgive them...*"

Christ was put in the incomprehensible situation of carrying the weight of everyone's sin and then moving to the next stage of complete forgiveness.

"*Forgive them...*"

That's what he did.

BUT I'M SCARED

Forgiving someone means giving up control—and because of our sinful nature, we resist that, don't we?

Forgiving someone also means we choose to walk in freedom according to God's will and not our own, and for some of us, that can be scary.

What kind of balancing act should there be when it comes to our desire to control the situation and our desire to have a Godly relationship? Which one intrigues you more?

Let's tackle the first idea of holding on to the reins and refusing to forgive someone. What does that mythical idea of control look like for you?

For me, there was a time in my life when I had held on to things people said about me for way too long—15 years too long. I subconsciously believed the lie that if I held on to the hurt, bitterness, and anger their statements caused me, then I would have some type of mystical power over them. In turn, they would have the same type of miserable life that I was having. Here's a side note: it just doesn't happen that way because they have already moved on.

This belief was a major factor in the depression and anxiety that began to overwhelm my life. I turned inward on myself allowing these deep-seated feelings to fester. I withdrew from friends and family, and loneliness, guilt, and shame became my best friends.

Over time, I began to understand that the only person I was controlling was myself.

In September of 2022, the Holy Spirit tapped me on my shoulder and encouraged me to release these individuals, to release myself from my own prison of unforgiveness.

After praying about it, I took out several sheets of blank paper, one for each person I needed to forgive. In the top right corner, the date was added and each letter was specifically addressed to one person who hurt me and they looked something like this.

Dear _____,

I need to let you know that when you said, or did, _____, it really hurt me. On this date, I choose to forgive you. I choose to move on and place this matter at the foot of the cross. It is no longer my burden to carry because Christ has already taken care of the matter.

Your name.

Each letter was folded in thirds and placed inside an envelope with their first names on it. When licking the envelope, I was slightly reminded of the hurt once again because of the awful taste of that sticky glue, but I continued. There were about ten letters altogether now stacked in a neat pile on my office desk. I left them there for three days, not paying any attention to them because I needed to be sure this was what I wanted to do. On the third day, I took the unstamped letters to a nearby drive-up mailbox. The drivers in the cars behind me seemed to grow a little impatient with me as I prayed over the letters one last time. The prayer went something like this, "Lord, again, I choose to forgive each of these people because your word commands me to do so and because I want to. I now place this whole matter of forgiveness in both your hands and the hands of the Postmaster." All the letters were slowly put into the slot the blue mailbox offered.

When driving away, for the first time in 15 years, I felt free. There was a brand-new joy that encompassed me along with a brand-new smile on my face. The weight of unforgiveness had been completely removed.

When we step out in faith the size of a mustard seed and face the very beast of unforgiveness that has controlled every facet of our lives, we learn that we can slowly begin to breathe again. We can begin to walk in new-found peace and joy because the chains become unlocked, and we are no longer prisoners of our own demise. The smile our friends and family used to see is returning—and now reflects peace. We can now understand that just as Christ forgave us, we too can forgive others.

The Mayo Clinic published an article, *Forgiveness: Letting go of grudges and bitterness*, and it lists the following benefits of forgiving someone: healthier relationships, improved mental health, less anxiety, stress, and hostility, fewer symptoms of depression, lower blood pressure, a stronger immune system, improved heart health, and improved self-esteem.[5]

I like what the Mayo Clinic had to say regarding the benefits to our mental and physical health but I'd like to add the following benefits for our spiritual health.

Restores our fellowship with God – Isaiah 1:18

Brings inner peace and joy – Psalm 32:1-2

Restores relationships – Ephesians 4:32

Sets us free from bitterness – Mark 11:25

We receive God's mercy – James 2:13

Leads to spiritual growth – Colossians 3:13

Brings God's blessings, mercy, and refreshing presence – Matthew 5:7

When reading over the lists just mentioned, did you notice anything peculiar? These benefits are great, but they are very one-sided. Did you observe that each of the mental, physical, and spiritual benefits of forgiveness is for the person who does the forgiving? Don't get me wrong, the act of forgiveness can and should be mutual so relationships might be fully restored, but if that cannot or does not happen, those who have been wronged need to move on.

We need to forgive the offender—without any expectations.

We need to heal.

Just in case the above-mentioned lists haven't swayed you enough to forgive others, here's a strong reminder from the Lord.

"For if you forgive other people when they sin against you, your heavenly Father will also forgive you. But if you do not forgive others their sins, your Father will not forgive your sins." Matthew 6:14-15

It's easy to forgive others when it applies to simple things like showing up a few minutes late or forgetting to put the dishes in the dishwasher. What about the bigger issues that cause hurt, trauma, or PTSD? What about those who have mentally, physically, or spiritually abused us? Are we to forgive them as well? According to what we just read in Matthew 6, Christ is letting us know that if we don't forgive the person who sins against us in any fashion, then our Heavenly Father will not forgive us. I'm not sure I can live with that, can you?

This next part of this chapter can be a little tough because it's another step in releasing the mythical control we talked about earlier.

Let's talk about the offender.

What happens to them?

Who will hold them accountable, if not you?

The only thing I can say is "It's not your responsibility to hold the person who has offended you accountable." It's God's responsibility. This is where your faith is going to be challenged and you have to trust God to do what He says He will.

There is a benefit for the offender, but only if they repent, according to 1 John 1:9,

"If we confess our sins, he is faithful and just to forgive us our sins and to cleanse us from all unrighteousness."

But you might say, "That's not what I want to have happen to the person who offended me."

Doesn't matter.

God is a fair and just God. Just like Christ forgave you of your sins, he can forgive the sins of your offender, and unfortunately, you have no say in that matter. I know that's a harsh way of truthfully looking at the grace God gives, but it's not inclusive to only those who have been offended. Look at the lists mentioned earlier. Study them. Read them out loud. Memorize them if you need to, but please do yourself a huge favor and begin to forgive the people who offended you.

As for me and the people who offended me, I forgave them. It took me several days, but after praying about the situations and the people, I forgave them. It doesn't mean I now have a bright and shiny halo, by no means. What it does mean, though, is that I no longer walk in anger or bitterness towards those people. When I finally forgave, my burden was lifted and I was set free from the unforgiveness cage that held me captive for so long. True freedom is not in holding on, but in letting go. Jesus forgave me, so I must forgive.

POINTS TO PONDER

Here is one last list and one last point I'd like to share.

A quick Google search on forgiveness leads to an article from *Psychology Today*, which explores three main topics: *How to Forgive Others*, *How to Forgive Yourself*, and *The Benefits of Forgiveness*[6]

Two of these are very helpful, but there is one that is completely unbiblical, *How to Forgive Yourself*. Their premise is that if we do something wrong towards ourselves, and once we realize that fact, we should apologize to ourselves for what we did, said, or thought. The concept is great for the secular culture we live in; however, it panders to individuals who are reluctant to embrace a relationship with Christ as their Savior. Internalizing our problems is what got us in trouble in the first place; therefore, forgiving ourselves has no merit whatsoever.

The conflict I have with the article is Biblically, there is nothing to support its position.

Chip Dodd, in his book *The Voice of the Heart*, challenges the common idea of self-forgiveness:

> Ironically, our society has taught us that we can forgive ourselves. (Hence, the Psychology Today article) The idea that I can forgive myself is a delusion of grandiosity and arrogance that damages all of my heart's hunger for intimacy. Forgiving myself makes me a god. This delusional belief screams arrogance because it is an attempt to become a god through my own self-sufficiency. There is no such thing as someone forgiving oneself.[7]

He goes on to clarify the above statement.

> I can only be forgiven by another or by God. I can't crawl up into my lap and say, "Chip, I'm sorry I did this to me." However, I can acknowledge that I treat myself terribly and

irresponsibly, and that I need to ask God and others to forgive me and help me. When I attempt to forgive myself, I am really in need of no one. I am denying my need for others or God to do for me what I cannot do.[8]

I can't stress enough how important it is to know that only God can forgive, as mentioned in Mark 2:7. While the idea of self-forgiveness may bring a temporary sense of relief, Scripture is clear: true forgiveness comes only from God. As 1 John 1:9 reminds us:

"*If we confess our sins, he* (Christ Jesus) *is faithful and just to forgive us our sins and to cleanse us from all unrighteousness.*" (emphasis added)

Rather than relying on ourselves for forgiveness, we are called to turn to God, our Faithful and Forgiving Redeemer. When we humbly go before our Heavenly Father, we are relinquishing every aspect of control when it comes to forgiveness. We are saying, "God, you know how to handle this 'forgiveness-situation' better than I do. I'm trusting you and not myself."

Before you read this chapter, what did the concept of 'redemption' mean to you?

Did you gain any more insight into 'redemption' after reading this chapter? If so, take time to write that down in your journal.

What examples can you reflect on that show how Christ has 'redeemed' your life? Jot down as many as you would like.

We are led to believe that 'forgiveness' comes with so many different components, yet, from a biblical standpoint it might not be as difficult as we make it out to be. What specifically stood out to you as you read through the section on 'forgiveness'?

Were you surprised that you can hold yourself prisoner by not forgiving others? Describe the difference between staying captive versus being set free.

Here's the tough question. Are there people in your life, past or present, that you need to walk through forgiveness with? What would it look like for you to begin the journey of forgiving them so you can walk in the peace and joy Christ provides us?

Would you feel comfortable creating a list of those you need to forgive, then praying and asking the Holy Spirit to reveal to you how to move forward in forgiveness?

At the end of the book, I've provided an email address. If you are comfortable sharing, I would love to read your stories of how, through Christ, you walked in faith to forgive others in your life and how you are now walking in freedom.

I am Forgiven Screensaver

Chapter Nine

I Am God's Child

*Yet to all who did receive him,
to those who believed in his name,
he gave the right to become children of God.*

John 1:12

As mentioned before, my wife and I have two sons who are now in their early twenties. Even though they are grown men doing quite well on their own, my wife and I still say each one is our child, or collectively, they are our children. In fact, my wife still lovingly refers to them as her babies.

As their mother and father, it is without doubt that we can easily say how proud we are of the young men they have become and the wonderful daughter-in-law we have.

Just like any family, we've had a lot of great times and there have been moments where life just was not working out so well for us. That's my kind way of saying things in our family were extremely difficult at times. Or, if I can once again quote my good friend, Eze, "Life can be like a blender set on high with the lid off."

It's been amazing to watch our family story unfold, especially as it pertains to our boys. As a dad I've had the incredible opportunity, when I was much younger, to get down on the living room floor and wrestle with my boys. There were tickle fights, playing catch, board games, and quite a number of hours playing video games.

I remember one particular time when our oldest son was about two years old. We were on all fours on the floor in the living room, and pretending to be lions. The contest was to see who could roar like a lion the loudest. I tried my best to sound like the alpha male but I think he won that day.

There was also the time my chest puffed up a couple of extra sizes when I watched my oldest son hit the baseball as high as possible, up and over our backyard fence into the back alley when he was around 6 years old. I'm not the guy you want on your baseball team, let alone pitching because I'm a terrible pitcher. But I remember pitching the ball to him, and then it happened. There was that once-in-a-lifetime moment between a father and his son. The ball was thrown and then I heard that CRACK which happens only when a dirtied old scuffed-up leather baseball meets a wooden bat being swung with purpose. Magic happened and it was all in slow motion from my standpoint. I remember looking up, higher and higher, watching the ball cut through the clouds eventually landing out of sight in the back alley. I looked back at my son to see the biggest smile on his face. What a proud moment we both shared.

Then, with my youngest son, the creative one, we would play for hours in the living room of our ranch-style home. Rummaging through his room, we found the huge tote full of foam blocks that came in all sorts of colors and sizes. Once they were brought to the living room we would dump the whole bucket on the floor. One by one we took turns, adding a new block to what we were building to see how high it could become before it toppled to the ground. I think the tallest foam block tower ever created was around four feet tall which was just as tall as he was at the time. Another proud moment.

Another great set of memories with my youngest son was spending time with him creating vivariums for his snake, lizards, and frogs. We would spend time at the local pet store buying the right glass display case, the plants, and pumps for the water feature. Hours were spent on Saturday mornings in our dining room cutting Styrofoam with a kitchen knife heated over the store so he could create different levels for this new home for his pets. By the way, he earned the money to pay for all of this. Okay, we helped out a little, but mostly, he earned the money.

I'd love to tell only the good stories—the times we laughed, played, and grew together. But that wouldn't be the full picture. Yes, there were birthdays, holiday gatherings with extended family, and huge vacations. Let's not forget the time I coached soccer, or went to their basketball and football games. There were numerous band concerts, and watching both of my boys in the marching band during half-time at all the football games in high school. These are the things I'd like you to remember about my family. My boys and I. Me being their father and them being my sons. The good stuff.

But there were also difficult times that often clouded over the good memories we had as a family.

With that in mind, I'd like to end the chapter right here giving you the illusion that our family was perfect in every way.

Oh, the urge is there, believe me.

However, by doing so, it would give a false narrative about some of the things that did happen in our family.

Just as we celebrate the highlights, we must also acknowledge the struggles. Being part of a family means experiencing both joy and hardship. My family was no exception, and there were years when our story was far from picture-perfect.

Here's an example of the challenging years that our family experienced.

In 2008, we packed up our family and moved an hour and a half away from friends and family. I took a new job in sales and my wife was still working on the weekends back in the city we just left. After a few short months, I lost my job as the recession of 2009 took off in full force.

Talk about a faith builder.

Even though our boys were doing well in their new school and I had found another job in sales, something still wasn't right.

I'm not sure exactly how to explain it but everything within our family life began to take a nose dive. Actually, everything in my life began to take a nose dive.

For whatever reason, I went into a huge devastating tail-spin of major depression and anxiety. There were too many hospitals, doctors' visits, and therapy appointments to remember which were all supposed to help me cope with this new diagnosis. Each day I felt less and less like a father, husband, man, and person. I was getting lost in a whole other world and I couldn't find the road map to help get me back home.

This went on for years.

My wife and our children watched me go from a fun-loving, happy-go-lucky, "Skippy-the-Dog-outlook-on-life" kind of dad to someone that just wanted to be isolated in a dark corner and sleep all day.

During those years I lost my job again along with my dignity, and most of all, the connection with my wife and two sons. There was only one statement that stood out to me about my situation and who I was.

I *was* a failure.

I *felt* abandoned, alone, guilty, embarrassed, and ill-equipped to handle life. Shame controlled every thought at that time. It was daunting and overwhelming, and hope was nowhere in sight.

Did you notice anything about the last two sentences? There's a factual confirming statement, "...*I was*..." and then there's a touchy-feely statement, "...*I felt*..."

How is it possible to experience two different conflicting points of view at the same time? There were vague memories in the dark and foggy recesses of my mind of who I was supposed to be and that my identity was straight from my Heavenly Father. Yet, when my life was spinning out of control, leaving me in a place of complete despair, it was easy to forget about the foundation my life was supposed to have been built on.

I've since reconciled with my two boys and we are working on healing the hurts from years gone by. I'm working on moving from a dad to a father with them.

THE BEGINNING

My wife and I received a certificate of authenticity for each of our boys called a birth certificate. In addition to that piece of paper, I was in the delivery room when each of them was born, so I can attest that they belong to us.

If you think about it for a moment, before we were ever formed, God was writing more than an official document for us. I can imagine God sitting at

His heavenly desk, "creating" every single detail and writing a book about us. He was not only the one forming us, but he was the author of all the details about what our lives would be like, and he wrote it all down in a book. A book with our names on it. A book with your name on it.

"Your eyes saw my substance, being yet unformed. And in Your book they all were written, the days fashioned for me, when as yet there were none for me." Psalm 139:16

My wife and I may have received a record of our son's birth from the hospital, but everyone ever born has had a book written about them by the Author of the universe. That trumps a birth certificate any day of the week if you ask me.

Not only did God write a book about us but he put a grandfathering clause in the fine print that says on the day we accept Christ as our Lord and Savior, we can begin to embrace the more than 284 identities he has for us. Try putting all those identities on a name badge and wearing that to work.

One of those identities is

"We are God's Child."

"Behold what manner of love the Father has bestowed on us, that we should be called children of God!" 1 John 3:1

That's who we really are.

I am God's Child.

You are God's Child.

At that moment when you dropped to your knees in a humble prayer of forgiveness and invitation, there was a song of rejoicing heard in the heavenly realm that announced your entrance into a very special family.

Can you imagine the look on your Heavenly Father's face when He turned and heard your sweet humble whisper or the loud declaration shouting out, "Please forgive me and come into my heart?"

Oh, the hallelujahs and amens must have been heard all around the throne. What an incredible time of celebration.

This is where it gets dicey though.

Some might make the argument that what has happened to them in their past, is what defines them. The imposing self-talk might sound like,

"But you don't know all the horrible things I've done in my life. God would never want to call me his child." Or, "The trauma and abuse I've experienced tells me I am not acceptable and God would never want me in his family."

Let's go out for coffee sometime and I'll share all the different ways I've messed up in my life. How I'm still messing up. We can compare notes. But, in the end, when it's all said and done, the truth still stands, if you have, or will, ask forgiveness of your sins and ask Christ into your heart, you have literally just become God's Child.

ACTIONS AND RESULTS

With what we've learned so far, how does this connect to John 1:12?

With further study, we find there is one key *action* and four *results* that are "...are short, simple and to the point addressing the beautiful transformation one experiences when applying this verse to their life."[1]

Receiving and Believing (Action)

To become a child of God, one must both *receive* Jesus and *believe* in His name. This is a personal action that involves a personal acceptance and trust in who Jesus is and what He has done.

Can I admit that I love getting gifts? There's something about ripping the paper off to see what's underneath it. When gifts are handed to you, did you ever consider the debt on that gift had already been paid? Someone worked hard, saved up the money, took the time to look for the perfect gift, and then wrapped it up in a beautiful paper and topped it with a bow, all just for you. For the receiver, the gift is free. The givers are the ones who have invested in something to give to you.

For us, the gift of forgiveness of our sins is free, but the debt was paid by Christ dying on the cross.

He paid the price.

This is an active acknowledgment and embrace of Christ's lordship and salvation.

Receiving the gift is one thing, but believing is another. How many times have we received a gift that was beyond belief and we ask the question, "Is that really for me?" There is an assumption within the Christian church that anyone who has not yet accepted Christ into their lives should be itching at the chance to accept this invitation. I wish that were so. When reflecting on my own life—and listening to countless others—I've learned that many of us carry the weight of this thought: "I'm just not worthy of a gift that big."

Believing—even with faith as small as a mustard seed—means trusting that Jesus is the Son of God and that His death and resurrection provide the means for eternal life.

The Right to Become (Result)

The term "right" in our focus verse indicates authority or privilege. Believers are granted the authority to become children of God, a status that is not earned but given by grace.

This is a transformative power granted to all those who believe in Christ. This authority we have been given allows us to live in a manner worthy of our new identity in Christ. There is both a "right" and a "responsibility" described here. Upon accepting this free gift, we now have the "right" or "authority" to be responsible for becoming imitators of God, Ephesians 5:1-2.

Please,

please,

please...

understand this authority and privilege, this "right" is NOT something to lord over another. There is nowhere within this gift that even conveys an attitude of "I'm better than you." From my perspective, accepting this privilege puts me directly at the foot of the cross while allowing me to stand confidently because of whose I am.

Identity in Christ (Result)

As children of God, believers have a new identity. This identity is not based on earthly status or achievements but on their relationship with God through Jesus Christ.

Paul consistently writes of "being in Christ" and follows through with these references.

New Creation: *"Therefore, if anyone is in Christ, he is a new creation..."* [2]

Union with Christ: *"I have been crucified with Christ; it is no longer I who live, but Christ lives in me..."* [3]

Self-Perception: *"Believers are called to see themselves as God sees them – loved, chosen, and valuable."* [4]

Spiritual Adoption (Result)

The concept of becoming children of God speaks to the spiritual adoption believers experience. This adoption brings with it the rights and responsibilities of being part of God's family.

It is extremely important we understand our Spiritual Adoption is NOT based on our own merit, the job title we have, the amount of money we make, or the social status we have. This adoption is a gracious act of God, signifying a change in the believer's status and relationship with God. In Romans 8:15, a result of this adoption for the believers is being called to live in a manner that reflects their new identity: adopted as God's Child. This includes growing in faith, exhibiting the fruits of the Spirit, and sharing the love of Christ with others.

Living as Children of God (Result)

Believers are called to live in a manner that reflects their new identity. This includes growing in faith, exhibiting the fruit of the Spirit, and sharing the love of Christ with others.

Here is a really good example I have occasionally shared in the past with others. In September of 1981, I arrived at Lackland Air Force Base in San Antonio, Texas to start my basic training as an Airman in the United States Air Force. However, before I could get on a plane and then a bus to arrive at the base, something had to occur first. Several months before I and 50 or 60 other young men and women met in a large room that looked very official-like. It reminded me of a courtroom without all the benches where the spectators would sit during a trial.

We were put into rows with a few feet between each person. I remember a man dressed in a black judge-type robe walking in, very astute, and explained we were going to take The Oath of Enlistment, declaring we were signing up to protect the Constitution.

Even though I knew what I was doing, I do not think I understood the full picture of what was happening in my life.

On the day I swore allegiance to my country I took on a brand-new identity. I was no longer just a citizen of the United States, I was now an Airman in the United States Air Force. I had a new identity and purpose with all the benefits that came with that position.

When I arrived at the Gateway to the Air Force (Lackland Air Force Base) for basic training, there was the traditional shaving of all the hair on our heads and fitting us with a brand-new uniform, boots, and a bunk. I was now afforded any and everything the government could offer a young man in the military. As time progressed, I remember a sense of honor when wearing my dress blue uniform.

In between basic training and tech school, I was about to board a flight to go back home for a short Christmas break. Two amazing gifts happened that night all because of my uniform and my new identity. The first was an older gentleman who approached me and put out his hand to shake mine, "Young man" he said, "I want to thank you for your service." I cordially thanked him for his kind words and stood a little taller than before. The second gift that night was after taking my seat in economy class, a flight attendant approached me and asked if I would gather my things and follow her. Again, like a good Airman, I followed her directions. As she walked towards the front of the plane, I began to wonder what was happening. When she stopped, she turned to me and stated, "There was an empty seat available in first class and we would like to offer it to you for no extra charge."

That is what it is like to be welcomed into a family of believers. We are given a new look, a new identity, a new set of clothes, and a new outlook on life according to 2 Corinthians 5:17.

ACCEPTING THE GIFT

We have touched on this just a bit before but I feel it necessary to expand on the principle of accepting this gifting.

For those of us who have already accepted this gift, I say, "Super-duper, groovy, cool, cool." I can't wait to meet you when we all get to our Heavenly home. For those who are still curious think about this for a moment,

"Whoever believes on Him will not be put to shame." Romans 10:11

Shame is an evil monster that whispers in our ears all of the reasons why we cannot accept anything, even if it is free. This form of humiliation turns us against ourselves and forces us to "feel" the following

I feel embarrassed.

I feel disgraced.

I feel horrible.

I feel disconnected.

I feel unworthy.

Here's a thought, "...you don't feel your way into good behavior; you behave your way into good feelings."[5] Or, put a little differently, your feelings do not dictate your beliefs or behavior, instead, you believe and change your behavior first and then the feelings will soon follow.

I mentioned this quote in the Introduction but it bears repeating here, "We don't become a new person by changing our behavior; we discover the person we already are in Christ and behave accordingly."[6]

IDENTITIES vs TITLES

The last part of this verse, although just as important as the receiving and believing part, is where the new identity: *I am God's Child* comes into play. *"...to become children of God"* brings with it a much better clarification,

"...anyone living in full dependence on the heavenly Father, i.e. fully (willingly) relying upon the Lord in glad submission. This prompts God to transform them [us] into His likeness."[7]

When we willingly rely on God, believing in Him for a new life we are instantaneously transformed into His Child.

"The Spirit Himself bears witness with our spirit that we are children of God." Romans 8:16

1 John 3:1 says, *"See what great love the Father has lavished on us, that we should be called children of God! And that is what we are!"*

How many of us wake up each morning yearning for the next promotion? The next big sale? The next new relationship? How many of us crave the title of Supervisor, Manager, or CEO? The Star football or basketball athlete? Sales Rep of the Year? President of the HOA, or PTA Board. At the time of this writing my wife and I are proud grandparents to a rambunctious 3-month-old black lab named Vada. Then there are the titles of father, dad, husband, mother, mom, wife. Titles come and go—jobs, achievements, and roles change over time. But your identity as God's child is eternal. Who you are in Christ is not based on what you do, but on whose you are. They are subjective and can change at any given moment. Yet, we grab for that next dollar or position, that next title. Chase them all you want, but you will never be fulfilled until you accept the free gift Christ offers and begin to discover your new identity in a relationship with him.

I've talked with too many people in my life who have found complete disappointment because they tried to find their identity in "being something." Then the floor gave out from under their feet and they were completely lost. The lid came off their blender and things got messy really quickly.

Upon accepting the identity as God's Child, we come to understand it is permanent—and cannot be taken away. Because God is perfect in all His ways, He cannot change His mind and take away your adoption as a Child of His.

Therefore, when the trials come, and they will come, you will be able to stand firm in your faith based on your identity as God's Child.

Let the storms rage and crash upon the rocky cliffs spraying sea foam all around you. Because of your relationship with Christ, your life is built on the solid rock of Christ and will not crumble.

Earlier in the chapter I mentioned a book God wrote in for every person ever conceived. A book that only focuses on you, on your redemption story. Did you know there is another book that is just as important and could possibly have your name in it? For those who have accepted this amazing gift of salvation, your name is written in the Lamb's Book of Life according to Revelation 3:5.

"The one who is victorious will, like them, be dressed in white. I will never blot out the name of that person from the book of life, but will acknowledge that name before my Father and his angels."

His love for us is flawless and perfect.

It is compassionate and firm.

POINTS TO PONDER

I *was* a failure.
  Now, *I am* God's Child.
  I *was* isolated, disconnected, and confused.

Now, *I am* in a relationship with my Heavenly Father who knows no boundaries.

Life will still bring trials, but now I face them with confidence—not as someone lost or forgotten, but as God's beloved child. No matter what comes my way, I know this: I am His, and He will never let me go.

At any given point in your life, have you ever told yourself, "I am not worthy of such a gift", or "Everyone hates me and looks down on me, there is no way God would want me as his child?" Are there other thoughts, like these, that fill your memories?

After reading about this new identity, I am God's Child, how do you think those statements you just wrote down could change? What would you like to tell yourself now?

If you haven't stepped into a relationship with your Heavenly Father, what are the "I feel" statements that are holding you back from making that decision?

Can you take those "I feel" statements and turn them into "I believe" statements? If so, rewrite those "I feel" thoughts into "I believe" action statements.

Write down a few action steps that will allow you to purposefully and intentionally apply this Identity to your life.

I am God's Child Screensaver

Chapter Ten

I Am God's Friend

*I no longer call you servants,
because a servant does not know his master's business.
Instead, I have called you friends,
for everything that I learned from my Father
I have made known to you.*

John 15:15

Typing the word "Friend" in the Google search bar brings up 12,880,000,000 results within 0.40 seconds. Changing that over to "God's Friend" we get 1,120,000,000 results in 0.32 seconds.

In 1855, Joseph M. Scriven penned the Christian hymn "What a Friend We Have in Jesus" which focuses on you and me as God's Friend and we are able to take all our cares and sorrows to Him in Prayer.

When I was in second grade my teacher taught us two lines of the poem (in song form) written by Joseph Parry, "Make new friends but keep the old, one is silver and the other gold."

Michael W. Smith, and his wife Debbie, wrote the forever popular Christian song "Friends Are Friends Forever" back in 1983 for a dear friend who was moving away.

Then, in 2004, the Contemporary Christian music group, Phillips, Craig, and Dean, released the song "Friend of God" on their *Let the Worshipers Arise* album. This song mentions several attributes of the depth within the relationship Christ has with us, yet it does not explain how or why we are able to have this relationship with our Savior.

We'll talk more about that in just a bit.

Let's take a look at the word friend and find out what it means,

The first known usage of the word *friend* as a noun was before the 12th century, using the definition *one attached to another by affection or esteem*. Whereas the word *friend* used as a verb was introduced in the 13th century with the definition of *to act as the friend of*. It's interesting to note that a more recent definition of friend, as a verb, has been changed to the following, *to act as the friend of, to include (someone) in one's list of designated friends on a social media site*. Ah, yes, let's bring social media into the picture.

The definition of Friendship is rather simple,

the state of being friends, the quality or state of being friendly.[1]

Here's a list of some famous friends in the Bible:

Ruth and Naomi

David and Jonathan

Daniel and his three friends

Mary, Martha, Lazarus, and Jesus

Paul, Timothy, and Epaphroditus

FRIENDSHIPS

Talk about brain overload. That was a lot of factual information to start the chapter off with, right? I love factual linear information. It helps my analytical brain stay calm cool and collected. The boxes and file cabinets in my brain are perfectly placed in nice neat rows. These days, I forget which cabinet holds what information.

Friendships are not linear, and they definitely don't belong in a file cabinet. Our friendships should not be based on a set of directions that might come in a box from IKEA. Friendships should be fluid and ever-changing—flexible and full of both laughter and honest conversations that hold us accountable.

Friendships should breathe life into us.

I've heard it's good to have at least one good faithful, vulnerable, trustworthy, supportive, and encouraging friend in your life. Not an acquaintance that sends you a "heart" emoji on your latest social media post, but a true friend. That way during times of celebration or tough days, you would have someone who will cheer you on or walk alongside you providing whatever encouragement and support is needed for that moment.

My friend is Bill and I have shared a strong friendship for the past 38 years.

We met in college way back in the day when the wheel was still being invented, and something just clicked between the two of us. There's a standing joke between us that we know more about each other than our wives know about us. Though we live 3–4 hours apart, we've spent more hours on the phone than we could ever count. We've had phone calls where we cried with each other, listened intently during the difficult moments, and prayed for one another. We have gotten together for birthdays, weddings, fishing, sailing, 4-wheeling in the rain and mud, building a chicken coop in 110-degree heat, and vacations. The friendship Bill and I have definitely checked off all the boxes when it pertains to the definitions written earlier.

I've also built up deep, meaningful friendships with men I've met through The Redeemed Men's Ministry. These mighty relationships are founded on trust, vulnerability, and connection and there is a true desire to lift each other up in prayer, hold each other accountable, and laugh. Let me tell ya, there's quite a lot of laughter happening as well.

As powerful as human friendships are, Jesus offers something even greater. In John 15:15, He makes a bold statement that transforms the way we see our relationship with Him. Here we go from just a friend to having a brand-new identity as God's Friend.

There are a couple of noticeable benefits when we have a friendship with God. First, there's a clear shift—from a disconnected relationship, like that of a servant, to a connected one, where we are invited to know and understand our Heavenly Father's heart. That's a huge promotion if you ask me. We must recognize that a slave obeys out of fear. A servant works out of duty. A bond-servant follows out of love. But a friend is invited to know the heart of the Master

DIFFERENCES

Let's examine this verse a little deeper. When looking into the Greek for the word *servant* we find two opposing definitions:

(1) a slave - someone who belongs to another; without *any ownership rights* of their own.

(2) The opposing definition, this definition is used with the *highest dignity* in the New Testament – namely, of believers who *willingly* live under Christ's authority as His devoted followers.[2]

The first definition for servant is where a person comes under the ownership of another. All their rights as a person have been stripped away and they have become a slave to their master. It was not uncommon in the New Testament days for a person who could not pay back a debt to become a slave to the one he owed the debt to. Someone, a friend or family member, had to pay the debt for that person before they would become free once again.

As a slave, you might work for a set period of time to repay your debt, have a portion forgiven each day, or—in the worst case—serve as a slave for life.

As a slave, you either worked for a specific time frame to pay off the debt, or the master of the house would take a little off your debt for each day you worked, or, in the worst case scenario, you became a slave for the rest of your life. Either way, the one ruling over you set the terms and conditions for you. There was nothing you could say or do to change their mind.

Being a servant, or a slave is task-oriented based upon the orders, demands, or wishes of the master. There is no connection of worth, identity, or love. It's just simply "do this" or "do that".

There is no relationship.

The outward manifestation of sin has control over the person to the point they have become a slave to the consequences of their behavior. Living as a servant to sin means being trapped—controlled by addiction, shame, or fear. They are a servant of sin. But Jesus offers freedom, calling us from slavery into friendship with Him. He doesn't just free us; He invites us into a relationship with Him.

However, when looking at the second definition, we find a completely different concept. In this case, a person is willfully submitting themselves to Christ's authority and accepting all He has to offer, thus becoming a bond-servant. This is based on a relationship because the debt, through Christ, has already been paid in full.

Imagine with me that you are in a relationship and you have been given full rights to all the attributes, character, and plans the master has for you. He freely gives his love to you through an overabundance of grace, mercy, and forgiveness. He accepts you as one of his own and calls you to sit at the same table with him.

That's what a relationship with Christ is all about.

What a significant difference between the two definitions.

One controls you while the other sets you free.

TRUST

For me to willingly submit to something or someone, there's a whole lot of trust that has to happen. I've been hurt too many times in my life to just willy-nilly trust someone. Maybe you have experienced that as well. When I put my faith in Christ years ago, there was a moment where I questioned the decision I was about to make. Am I ready to trust someone I've never met before or do I have enough faith to accept the incredible plan God has for my life?

Christ died a horrific death on the cross for the sins of the world. For me. For you. He paid the ultimate price and paid off ALL of the debts every one of us has ever been charged with. Then, Christ does something the Old Testament authors wrote about and those in the time of the New Testament were still learning about, He offered us a FREE gift.

He offered us the opportunity to have the chains broken and no longer live as a slave, but through His gift, we now become His friends.

Ultimately, though, I had to decide whether I wanted to continue as a slave to sin or become a bondservant to Christ and be his friend. Thankfully I chose the latter.

Here's a verse that literally breaks down the walls of any type of stereotypical thought of being a Child of God.

> *So, in Christ Jesus you are all children of God through faith, for all of you who were baptized into Christ have clothed yourselves with Christ. There is neither Jew nor Gentile, neither slave nor free, nor is there male and female, for you are all one in Christ Jesus.*[3]

With that verse in mind, I feel as if I should just end the chapter right here. We're done. What more is there to say?" "...for you are all one in Christ Jesus." That is, for those who have become a bond-servants to Christ. If you have accepted Christ as your personal Lord and Savior, asking forgiveness of your sins, and are living for the Lord, you are, "...one in Christ."

But, wait, there's more.

Earlier in the chapter we looked at the definition of *friend* and *friendship* from what the Merriam-Webster's Dictionary had to say. Now, let's look at what the Word of God has to say.

Looking at the Greek definition of the word *friend*, we learn the following:

a friend; someone *dearly* loved (prized) in a personal, intimate way; a trusted *confidant*,[4]

As we read through that definition, it's important to notice the depth of what Paul is referring to as it pertains to *friend*. This type of relationship is more than who knows our names and talks about our jobs. This trusted confidant is a *close friend or associate to whom secrets are confided or with whom private matters and problems are discussed.*[5]

To be seen as *dearly loved* and a *trusted confidant* is something some of us might not feel comfortable with. Because of the life experiences we have faced, we don't deserve to be welcomed into such a friendship with God. Stay on the outside and play it safe. That's what we are supposed to doing because we either do not *feel* worthy to be considered God's friend or we stumble with the question of "Doesn't being a friend of God put me on the same level as God?" Absolutely not. I know of no way we can ever be on the same level as God – our Creator. That's already been tried before and it didn't work out so well for the angel that was cast out of heaven. According to John 15:16, Christ says the following, "You did not choose me, but I chose you..." therefore, as believers we are called God's Friend.

Christ has already taken the first step towards you by inviting you to be his friend. He values you so much and is calling you from a life as a slave to a brand new life as his friend.

Therefore, to be considered a "friend of God" is different than something like the relationship between David and Jonathan or Paul, Timothy, and Epaphroditus. Don't get me wrong, these were powerful and deep friendships. They were so strong that the writers of the Old Testament and the New Testament found it important to record these relationships more than 2,000 years ago to have them as an example for us today. There is a defined strength with each of these individuals and their part in the relationship, but being a friend of God is completely different. It means that *"Our identity in Christ transforms from mere servants to beloved friends, which should impact how we live and serve."*[6]

This is an expansion of what Jesus is saying in John 15 when he says, "I no longer call you servants." Here Jesus is actually speaking about the change of relationship.

There are two keywords in Ephesians 1:7: redemption and forgiveness.

In Him we have redemption through His blood, the forgiveness of sins, according to the riches of His grace. (NKJV)

Christ's redemptive work on the cross not only provided complete forgiveness of our sins— it also fully paid our debt.

These are two specific and purposeful actions that Christ resolved on our behalf so we could move from being a slave to bond-servant. Think about it for a moment. Jesus didn't just rescue us from slavery—He calls us friends. He stepped into our world so we could step into His. The invitation is open: Will you walk in that friendship today?

POINTS TO PONDER

Four major components are happening John 15:15.

Without Christ we would continue to be in a master/servant relationship with the world having absolutely no rights whatsoever.

With Christ we could willfully choose to be in a relationship where we are invited to sit at the table with Christ and learn what it means to be a friend of God.

We can recognize that the only way the transition from servant to friend can happen is through the sacrificial gift Christ gave us through his death on the cross.

We can make a daily decision to follow biblical principles make our lives to reflect more of Christ than the world.

Describe in a few words what your life was like, or is like as a slave to sin with the chains still intact and holding you as a prisoner.

John 15:15 says, "You did not choose Me, but I chose you." Write down what it means to you to be *chosen* by Christ Himself."

What is the impact on your life knowing that as a friend of God you are *dearly loved*, a *trusted confidant*, and God sees your *value*?

Write down the names of three people you know who need to hear about the message that breaks the chains of the past so they can walk in a present and future life with Christ because they are loved, trusted, and valued.

Now, write down an action plan of how you will share this message of redemption and forgiveness with them.

Write down a few action steps that will allow you to purposefully and intentionally apply this Identity to your life.

I am God's Friend

Chapter Eleven
I Am Made by God

*For we are God's handiwork,
created in Christ Jesus to do good works,
which God prepared in advance for us to do.*

Ephesians 2:10

I don't remember how old I was when I went to Camp May Mac just outside of Lake Tahoe, CA, but there are a lot of memories to be had. For two weeks in the middle of summer, we learned about archery, how to make a campfire, learned new songs, and made a lot of friends.

The first time I went to Camp May Mac I didn't know what to expect so I just followed along with the other kids and my camp counselor to the next scheduled event. By the way, my counselor's name was Tall Pine. Well, that was his nickname, and yes, he was really tall, especially to a bunch of highly-spirited young boys who all slept in a teepee. I liked a lot of the activities at camp but one event that stood out to me was when we made crafts.

One particular day we were given a mound of wet slimy cold clay with the simple directions of "Make whatever you want." My little brain exploded with ideas and after a few short minutes, I had the perfect creation in mind. I made a Foot Vase.

Yep, you read that correctly. The vase was about 10" tall and 3" in diameter, and a foot was added to the bottom of it so it could be proudly put on any shelf or table displaying God's handiwork through flowers I would pick for my mom. There was quite a lot of laughter from the other campers and counselors about what I was making, but I stuck to my idea and loved every bit of the finished product.

What I didn't know was at the end of camp the counselors handed out various participation awards. Blue ribbons and certificates were being handed out like candy and all the kids were eating it up. I remember sitting there, on a huge log bench watching everyone else get something and feeling left out.

Then it happened.

The counselors handing out the awards called my name for me to come down in front of all the other campers. I was completely shocked. At that time in my life, I had already realized other kids get the prizes, not me.

Once I was in front of all the other kids, the camp counselors brought out my Foot Vase, which I had completely forgotten about, and handed it to me with a certificate. The certificate was for the most creative craft project for the whole two weeks. I was more than proud standing there in front of about a hundred other kids getting one of the best awards the camp could present. That was something the other kids couldn't take away from me.

It started with a thought, idea, or inspiration, which was worked into the clay. Molding, shaping, and painting were next followed by presenting it to the camp counselors. The final step was receiving a certificate for the best art project in front of all the other campers, a moment I am still proud of to this day because I *made* the vase.

There is a process here that I'd like us to investigate.

IDEA | CREATED IN CHRIST

This is a dual thought that leads back to God's unequivocal and profound plan for each of us, established before time. It highlights the value and purpose God infused into the design of not just the earth and all within it, but also the galaxies beyond. God's vision for us was established before we were conceived and is firmly rooted in His divine purpose for our lives.

Psalm 139 reveals that God designed every detail of our lives—our looks, personality, and purpose. While here in Ephesians 2:10, Paul identifies the purpose of why we were created. You see, we can have ideas all day long of what we want to do, or make, but without a reason or purpose behind the idea, that's all it is, an idea.

One of the main purposes behind God's idea of individually creating us was so our lives could be transformed, ...*created in Christ*... through a relationship with his Son.

"Therefore, if anyone is in Christ, he is a new creation; old things have passed away; behold, all things have become new." 2 Corinthians 5:17 (NKJV)

CREATION | GOD'S WORKMANSHIP

I have to admit that when I see the word "workmanship," I immediately think of hammers, drills, and lumber. Even though I am a very creative person, I never thought of "workmanship" as something artistic. Yet, through the ages, the Greek word Paul used for workmanship, *poiéma* means *something that has been made or created*.[1] This word has evolved from Greek to Latin, then to Old French, and finally into Middle English as the word *poem*, which we use today.

Ideas equal workmanship which equals creation and creation equals you and me.

When I read the creation story written in Genesis, unfortunately, I tend to think of it as black and white not considering the immense magnitude of creativity God used in making the universe and world we live in. Don't get me wrong, I am amazed at God's creation all around me. I've seen the Grand Canyon, beaches, oceans, prairies, and pictures of the vast galaxy we live in from the James Webb Telescope, but I can only understand a limited amount of God's full scope of creation. The point that I'm trying to make is God's depth of creativity and workmanship extensively steps outside the boundaries of hammers, drills, and lumber.

Rev. Timothy Keller made the following statement about the Holy Spirit and the scope of his workmanship,

> If the Holy Spirit is not only a preacher that convicts people of sin and grace but also a gardener, an artist, and an investor in creation who renews the material world, it *cannot* be more spiritual and God-honoring to be a preacher than to be a farmer, artist, or banker.[2]

The list of different types of creative people and things they have done in this world would be too long for this book. Yet, God has breathed into each one of us just what we need for the moment. God breathed into us his creativity, his design, and his imagination. C. H. Spurgeon helps us visualize this workmanship through this illustration.

> You have seen a painter with his palette on his finger and he has ugly little daubs of paint on the palette. What can he do with those spots? Go in and see the picture. What splendid painting! In an even wiser way does Jesus act toward us. He takes us, poor smudges of paint, and He makes the blessed pictures of His grace out of us. It is neither the brush nor the paint He uses, but it is the skill of His own hand which does it all.[3]

Just like I created the Foot Vase at summer camp and it became the result of my work, we were made by God and are considered His workmanship, His poem, His artistic masterpiece.

PRESENTATION | FOR GOOD WORKS

It's my careful assumption that everything created has a purpose. Whether it's the dirt in our backyard for growing a garden, or a sharp scalpel used in surgery, everything—big or small—was made for a reason. If not, then why was it created?

The moment we invited Christ into our lives, the transformation described in 2 Corinthians 5:17 began. *Instantly*, we became a new creation in Christ. That transformation is just one example of the exceptional work God does in our lives. And one way we reflect that transformation—one way we represent Christ to the world—is by doing the good works He prepared for us in advance.

"*Danger! Danger! Warning, Will Robinson.*"

Do you remember this line from the TV show "*Lost in Space*"? The fact that the robot in that show could always sense danger well before the Robinson family could. That always amazed me. We need to follow suit and be extremely careful with this section of scripture. First of all, no, I am not suggesting we are robots but I do want to stress the importance of understanding our relationship with Christ is not based on "good works." Instead, it is because of the relationship we have with Christ that we are able to do the good works described in scripture.

Case in point,

"*So that you may live a life worthy of the Lord and please him in every way: bearing fruit in every good work, growing in the knowledge of God.*" (emphasis added) Colossians 1:10

This verse explains that through the cross, Christ redeemed us so that we can do what is good and pleasing to him by bearing fruit (good works) that reflects the one we belong to. We recognize that because of Christ in our lives, we are to "*...do good works.*" The next set of verses describes what these good works might look like.

"*...let your light shine before others, that they may see your good deeds before others, that they may see your good deeds and glorify your Father in heaven.*" Matthew 5:16 (emphasis added)

"*In everything set them an example by doing what is good...*" Titus 2:7

"*And let us consider how we may spur one another on toward love and good deeds.*" (emphasis added) Hebrews 10:24

It is good to volunteer at the local food bank, the hospital, and the church but those good works do not get us to heaven. If we do not have the time, we may financially support various causes, but once again, that in no way means we are getting through pearly gates.

While Scripture calls us to good works, culture often tries to redefine them. We're told what causes to support, what beliefs to adopt, and even how to measure our worth. But God—not the world—defines our purpose.

But let me ask: Are you still listening to the messages you grew up with? You know, the ones that tell you you're an idiot. "How stupid can you be?" What about the name-calling on the playground at school or the hurtful messages you may have received while at church?

All these types of thoughts influence us in how we present ourselves to others, confident or insecure. The opinions and judgments of others can shape how we choose to serve—and sometimes, they can misguide our understanding of what good works truly are.

Our culture and past opinions of ourselves can hold us back from embracing the full impact of who we are in Christ. Some of us, no wait, a lot of us have become lost in what others think we should be doing. We seem to constantly be trying to gain approval and acceptance, but are only spinning our wheels and going nowhere.

I encourage you to tune out what "they" say and begin embracing who God says you are, *Made by Christ*. By recapturing your true identity in Christ, you now have a purpose for doing good works so you can be an example for others, helping them move from the darkness into his marvelous light.

RECOGNITION | PRESENTING US

I couldn't wait to get home and show my mom my Foot Vase and certificate. The bus ride seemed slow and monotonous taking forever to reach our destination. Before my mom could ask "How was camp?" I burst into the headline news of my vase. Even though it was packed deep in my suitcase, protecting it from any bumps along the way, I wanted my mom to drive as fast as possible so we could get home so I could show her my pride and joy. My gift to her.

After God created the world we live in, Genesis 1:31 says, *"God saw [all] that he had made, and it was very good…"* (emphasis added).

The author of Isaiah 43:7 says, *"Everyone who is called by my name, [whom I created for my glory,] whom I formed and made."* (emphasis added)

And then there is one of my favorite verses, Zephaniah 3:17, *"The Lord your God in your midst, the Mighty One, will save; He will rejoice over you with gladness, He will quiet you with His love, He will rejoice over you with singing."*

If the typical camp counselor could recognize my craftsmanship, how much more does our perfect Creator delight in us—His true masterpiece? What kind of thoughts do you think your Heavenly Father has towards you right now? This exact moment in time. What would he be saying to you, his creation? What would you like Him to say?

Dennis Jernigan is a singer-songwriter of contemporary Christian music who has inspired me for more than thirty years. Here is a portion of how he interpreted Zephaniah 3:17. I have changed the pronouns from "you" and "your" to "me" and "my" so as you read this text, it becomes personalized just for you. I would also encourage you to read this aloud so you can hear the affirming message from this powerful passage.

> *He has come to set me free,*
> *to keep me safe and bring me to victory.*
> *He is cheered and He beams with exceeding joy*
> *and takes pleasure in my presence.*
> *He has engraved a place for Himself in me*
> *and there He quietly rests in His love and affection for me.*
> *He cannot contain Himself*
> *at the thought of me and with the greatest joy*
> *spins around wildly in anticipation over me...*
> *and has placed me above all other creations*
> *and in the highest place in His priorities.*
> *In fact, He shouts and sings in triumph*
> *joyfully proclaiming the gladness of His heart*
> *in a song of rejoicing!*
> *All because of me!*[4]

Wait a minute.

The same God that created the whole universe and beyond, the One who *made you* (his workmanship) is in your midst and will save you. He rejoices over you with gladness, quiets you with His love, and rejoices over you with singing.

It is also important to remember that Christ is our Advocate and is constantly interceding for and presenting us before our Heavenly Father.

"My dear children, I write this to you so that you will not sin. But if anybody does sin, we have an advocate with the Father – Jesus Christ, the Righteous One." 1 John 2:1

and

"Who then is the one who condemns? No one. Christ Jesus who died – more than that, who was raised to life – is at the right hand of God and is also interceding for us." Romans 8:34

The one who made us delights in who we are because he is the one who created us. Because of our sinful nature, Christ has become both our Advocate and an Intercessor for us, *presenting* us before the Father. God does not need reminding of who we are, yet, because of the absolute purest compassion Christ has for us, he continually confirms us as redeemed before his Father, before our Father.

PROUD OF THE WORK | IT IS GOOD

There were too many red lights on the day we were driving back from camp. Even though the bus driver drove the speed limit it just wasn't fast enough for this young boy. Mom did the same, obeying all the traffic signs and lights. On the way home from the drop-off location the streets and highways were filled with every make and model of vehicle, all taking their time.

There was a rush of excitement the moment Mom put the car in park under the carport roof. The seat belt came off and the door flew open. My only thought was running to the back of the car to get my suitcase out of the trunk. The trunk lid couldn't be opened fast enough for me to grab my suitcase full of dirty clothes and my prized possession.

Where's the zipper? Ugh, it's stuck. Try it again. It's open—grass-stained smelly clothes flying everywhere.

There it is.

The Foot Vase and certificate.

I carefully picked it up, beaming from ear to ear and slowly turned to my mom relinquishing my handiwork. Then finding the certificate, that now looked a little worn, I recounted the story of how I was called up to the front of all the campers to receive this prestigious award.

When looking at the Foot Vase, Mom's expression was at first that of curiosity, as in, "I've never seen a foot vase before." But the smile on her face as she placed it on a shelf in the living room for family and friends to see was priceless. I felt valued and appreciated for the creative work that went into something I *made*.

IDEA | PREPARED IN ADVANCE

Every creation has two parts—the act of making it and the purpose it will serve. One portion of the *idea* has an immediate effect on the item being created while the other attempts to define the long-term usage, all of which must go into the planning stages before the item is created.

There is still one last important phrase in Ephesians 2:10 that we need to look at and it is *"...prepared in advance..."*

Here's an example of how I used to prepare for our family vacations in advance.

Typically, my wife and I would save up our money to pay cash for a huge family vacation which usually involved a cruise ship to the Bahamas. We immediately began putting money into a special savings account with the promise of not touching it until it was time to pay our deposit. We needed passports so pictures were taken and applications filled out. As we got closer to the cruise date our small family of four gathered around the dining room table, with one small laptop, and began picking out the excursions we were interested in. Then there was purchasing the plane tickets and hotel rooms. We even planned for souvenirs and t-shirts.

These trips were a time when our family could get away from the everyday stress of life and just have fun. But, just like it says in Ephesians 2:10, we "...prepared in advance..." for our trip.

God prepared everything about our lives before the beginning of time.

"For I know the plans I have for you," declares the LORD, "plans to prosper you and not to harm you, plans to give you hope and a future." Jeremiah 29:11

Think of it this way, he already knew about the difficult times you would face and prepared you specifically for them. The celebrations in your life, yep, he knew about them as well and brought the right friends and family to your side to commemorate with you.

To fully grasp this short phrase we need to recognize God's sovereignty, that He is in control, and know that ultimately His plans are good. There is hope when we put our trust in his plan for our lives. Within this relationship we are guaranteed the opportunity to prosper, but not as the world defines. When living with our purpose in Christ, we need to understand our prosperity focuses on spiritual growth and eternal blessings.[5]

You are not an accident. You are God's masterpiece—designed, crafted, and prepared for a purpose only you can fulfill. So go forward, not as a product of chance, but as a work of divine artistry—created to reflect His glory in the world.

POINTS TO PONDER

What an absolute privilege it is to be created by God himself so that within a redemptive relationship with his son Jesus Christ, we gain freedom from our past. What an absolute honor it is to have a life transformed into a new creation so that we can walk in a manner worthy of glorifying Christ through the good works he has already planned out for us before the beginning of time.

Take a few minutes to reflect on this chapter by answering the following questions.

Write down something you created. Describe your process and how you felt when it was completed.

What comes to mind when you read that God gave you the breath that brought you to life, instilled within you a divine inspiration, and to top it off, gave you the intelligence to accomplish good works for Him?

You are definitely more important than a Foot Vase to God. What does it mean to you to be God's workmanship?

Knowing God took special care to create every part of who you are, how does that motivate you to have a deeper relationship with Him?

Write down an action plan of at least three "good works" you can accomplish that will be a reflection of who Christ is in you. What are they, when will you put them into action, and how are you looking to be a reflection of this?

I am Made by God Screensaver

Chapter Twelve

I Am an Overcomer

For everyone born of God overcomes the world.
This is the victory that has overcome the world, even our faith.
Who is it that overcomes the world?
Only the one who believes that Jesus is the Son of God.

1 John 5:4 – 5

Wouldn't you agree that there are many ways to imagine what it means to be an Overcomer.

My first thought is some tough guy free-climbing Yosemite's Half Dome and making it to the top without any problems.

Or, an amazing wife and mom trying to juggle a full-time job while caring for her kids, and keeping the house clean, all while putting dinner on the table seven nights a week and preserving her sanity.

Then there are the millions of people fighting some form of medical or mental illness. How about the men and women who are struggling to overcome an addiction? Maybe they've lost their job, family, and dignity.

We can't forget about the countless EMTs, Police, Firefighters, and Military personnel constantly putting their lives on the line for us. The level of stress can be daunting as they overcome each new day they face.

26.2

Looking back to August 1984 I still have distinct memories of when I ran the Omaha Riverfront Marathon. While running the race, I had two pivotal moments that I still reflect on periodically.

The first was just as I crossed the two-mile marker, I thought to myself, "What are you doing? Do you realize you're running a race that is 26.2 miles long? Are you crazy?" However, just as fast as I had those thoughts, I pushed them aside to focus on my pace and goal of finishing the race.

Then, several miles later, I fell into the trap that so many long-distance runners experience, I hit the wall. It's a mental place some runners go to around mile 18. Their body begins to rebel against them and say "This is no longer fun and I want you to stop. If you don't stop this ridiculous race, I will take revenge on you."

Two different types of runners emerge around the 18th mile, the one who fights through the body yelling at them and they keep running and the other is the one who slows down to a slow walk. On that beautiful day, I was the one who slowed down to a walking pace. I know I should have kept running, even if it was a slower pace, but... As other runners, that I had already passed, began to pass me, they shared words of encouragement such as, "Keep going. Don't give up." "You can do this." And, "You're almost to the finish line." Those words of encouragement kept me from quitting the race. Those words were significantly important to me then, and they still are today.

I'm not sure how far I walked but eventually, I gained enough mental fortitude and grit to start running again. I started nice and slow to get my body used to the torture I was putting it through. My leg muscles began crying out with intense pain, trying to make me stop again, but not this time. I had a goal of finishing the marathon even if I had to crawl across the finish line.

Eventually, I noticed more and more people were lining both sides of the street cheering on the runners. They were cheering me on. They wanted me to win my own personal race. Their cheers fed the adrenaline inside every fiber of my body, and I began to run faster. The further along I ran, there were more and more people gathering, clapping, shouting, and motivating the runners, motivating me.

As the encouragement escalated, the adrenaline increased and I began to run even faster than I did at the beginning of the race. This new level of energy spurred me on to the finish line.

That particular year, the organizers of the race decided to make a significant change to where the race would end. This was the first year they had the finish line inside the Omaha Coliseum and the only way to get to the finish line was to go through a tunnel. Why on earth is a tunnel so important? It's important because I began to imagine I was running in the Olympics, representing the USA. Mentally, as I ran through the tunnel of the Omaha Coliseum, it was like I was running into the huge Olympic stadium full of spectators and the feeling was intense.

Running still faster than I could ever imagine, I began to hear the crowd inside the event center. It was deafening and exciting. My running turned into sprinting. The people on the sides of the street became a blur as I forgot about them and focused on the finish line. I could hear the clapping and cheering but I no longer noticed the people. That last-minute sprint allowed me to cross the finish line with a time of 4:07:04. Not bad for my first and only marathon.

That day, I truly felt like an Overcomer—celebrating with a medal, a photo, and a vow to never run a marathon again.

You can't be an Overcomer unless there's something to overcome. In other words, you have to be fully engaged in some kind of activity before you can overcome it.

Case in point, the man climbing Half Dome, the mother of 3.2 children holding down a full-time job, people dealing with medical or mental illness, and those battling addiction, those on the front line every day mentally struggling with PTSD. Each one of these people are completely immersed in some type of activity they are *choosing*, or wanting to overcome. They may not like the fact that they have to overcome something, but they still decide to do something about the condition they are in.

There's another type of race everyone is involved in, but this time their soul is involved and heaven is the finish line. In 1 John 5:4 – 5, we find five key components that will help us become an Overcomer.

Radical Transformation – "...everyone born of God..."

Result – "...overcomes the world."

Resource – "...our faith."

Reminder – "Who then overcomes...?"

Relationship – "Only he who believes..."

Let's take a look at each one of these.

RADICAL TRANSFORMATION

Being *"...born of God..."* is a radical transformation that dramatically changes one's life immediately and for all eternity. The decision we make to follow Christ has both immediate and eternal implications. Since you are reading Chapter 12 of this book, you have already learned about eleven other identities in Christ that were automatically given to you when you were *"born of God."*

It's important to note, however, that there is a significant difference between being physically born and spiritually born.

When I was physically born in a hospital, way back in the day when the wheel was being invented, I belonged to my mom and dad. It was such a special day that the hospital gave my parents a certificate proving I belonged to them. Even though I'm sure I was the cutest baby ever born, this physical act of being born brought me into a sinful world, and there was nothing I could do about that.

Because sin entered the world when Adam and Eve disobeyed God, every one of us was born into a sinful world. Just like me, you can't do anything about that either.

At the age of nine, when at a church summer camp, I asked for forgiveness of my sins and invited Christ into my heart. At that very moment I was *"born of God."* According to Colossians 2:13-14, instantaneously all of my past, present, and future sins were forgiven. It is also important to note, "It is not the mere fact of having received this Divine birth..., but the permanent results *and benefits* of the birth *as well."* (emphasis added).

RESULT

Google states that approximately 1.1 million people finish a marathon every year. That means over the past 40 years, approximately 44 million people have run the race. I don't want to minimize the fact that I ran a marathon, but, in the grand scheme of things, so what? I *overcame* something the world had to offer. While completing a marathon is a personal victory, overcoming the world has far greater significance—it's an eternal triumph in Christ.

However, on an even larger scale, an eternal scale, a kingdom scale, I am important, and you are important. As believers in Christ, we have the assurance that in the end, we will see Christ and enter into his presence. Jesus makes the following statement in John 3:3, *"...Very truly I tell you, no one can see the kingdom of God unless they are born again."*

Regardless of what we face each day when we head out the door, on the kingdom level we have already *"... overcome the world."* Instead of running through a tunnel to receive an award, we are ushered through the heavenly gates as mentioned in Revelation 21 and 22 to live an eternity with our Savior.

The secondary part of this verse states that as a new creation in Christ we are to diligently accept the faith God gives us and actively walk in the transformative power rising above the cultural cries that are all around us. We are to put Philippians 4:13 to the test as we participate in the strength God gives us.

"I can do all things through him who gives me strength."

It is my belief that there is more power in one small act of faith for a man, woman, or child who walks with a Christ-like purpose than an entire army that has been set against them.

RESOURCE

Did you know that faith ... really isn't ours but it's something on loan to us from God — let me explain. I remember as a kid going to church and hearing the lesson about needing some level of faith to do even the simple act of sitting in a chair. Before we sit down, we must have faith that the chair will bear our weight without collapsing.

Many would say we get the faith to sit in the chairs from past experiences of sitting in a chair. Or, we've seen other people sitting in a chair, so, if it supported them, it will support us. This is an example of how faith is played out, yet, it doesn't address how we obtain the kind of faith to be an Overcomer.

So, where did faith originally come from?

Paul answers this question for us in Ephesians 2:8,

"For it is by grace you have been saved, **through faith – and this is not from yourselves,** *it is the gift of God."(emphasis added)*

and

"So then faith comes by hearing, and hearing by the word of God." Romans 10:17 (NKJV)

and

"Fixing our eyes on Jesus, the author and perfecter of [our] faith..." (emphasis added) Hebrews 12:2 (NASB)

Any amount of faith you are walking in right now has been a gift from God. Faith is the foundational piece to salvation which allows us to accept our new Identity in Christ. It is faith from God that allows us to overcome the world. He imbues us with faith out of love, revealed though His grace and mercy. Even though God gives us the gift of faith, it is up to each of us to accept the gift. Remove the bow and wrapping paper, and put the gift into action.

Hebrews 11 is a Hall of Fame example of those who have gone on before us and have shown what it is like to walk in God's precious gift.

By faith, believers understand God created the universe.

By faith, Abel brought God a better offering.

By faith, Enoch was taken from this life.

By faith, Noah built an ark.

By faith, Abraham moved his family, and, by faith, Sarah, in her old age gave birth to Isaac, who was offered to God as a sacrifice.

By faith, blessings were passed down from Isaac to Jacob and Esau.

By faith, the walls of Jericho fell because of Joshua's obedience.

By faith, Rahab, a prostitute, had her life spared because she welcomed spies into her home.

I'm guessing that you can look around you and recall people in your life who walked by faith. By seeing their faith in Christ, you can be encouraged to acknowledge the faith God was offering you and begin to walk, jog, run, or sprint toward the finish line.

REMINDER

We can answer the question of, "Who then *overcomes*...?" by acknowledging those who have accepted Christ as their Lord and Savior are the ones who have and are Overcomers. Within this relationship, we are never promised a physical life without trouble but we are promised an eternal life without trouble. Through the power of the Holy Spirit and the work of Christ in our lives, we would overcome some of these difficulties here on earth and all of them once we arrive home. There will be things we need to endure, experience, and grow through on this earth, but when we arrive at our Heavenly home, our focus will be completely different. It's there, that we will instantaneously be free from everything our sinful nature brought into our lives. There will be no more crying, pain, or sorrow.

"He will wipe every tear from their (our) eyes. There will be no more death or mourning or crying or pain, for the old order of things has passed away." (emphasis added) Revelation 2:15

That is a promise believers can look forward to. That is an eternal hope we carry in our hearts.

Relationship

"Only he who *believes*..." actually speaks about relationships with our Savior and other brothers and sisters in Christ.

The Greek definition of *believes* is *"have faith in, trust in"*[1] conveying a sense of trust and reliance upon someone or something and is often described as the act of believing in Jesus Christ for salvation, trusting God's promises, and having faith in the truth of the Gospel.

Did you notice the definition used here refers to having a personal connection with Christ? Nowhere in the Bible does it say we are to believe in the security of our jobs, titles, relationships, or our own desires. When we look outward, we see chaos and confusion. When we look upward, we experience peace, joy, forgiveness, and God's mercy. Through this relationship with God, we can grow in Christ inwardly, which then allows us to be an outward example for Christ.

This belief draws us into the full reality of Jesus' divine Sonship—affirming both His deity and His unique relationship with the Father (John 1:14, 18). There is more to this belief than an intellectual understanding of Greek or Hebrew and cultural contexts used throughout scripture. This belief involves absolute trust and reliance upon Jesus for every aspect of our current and eternal life.

POINTS TO PONDER

We all wear different shoes but we all are running a race. Waking up each morning there is no banner in our bedrooms to remind us of this race, we just instinctively know we're walking, jogging, running, or sprinting through this life in order to receive the prize of being an Overcomer.

Take time to celebrate the "wins" and mourn the "losses". Reflect on the prior victories and learn from the defeats.

Each small victory builds toward the ultimate triumph—the day we see Christ face to face. Until then, run the race with faith, knowing you are already an Overcomer in Him. One day, believers in Christ will cross heaven's finish line—not to the applause of a crowd, but to the open arms of Christ who endured the cross for us.

Knowing that being an Overcomer is an action we take based on the faith given to us by God, Himself, write down as many details as possible about the day you accepted Christ into your life.

How has your life changed or stayed the same because of your decision to follow Christ?

Describe one of the biggest challenges you had to overcome and how God's grace and sovereignty helped you get through it.

How have you been able to take that challenging moment and use it to increase your faith? Or, since God gave you the faith to originally walk through that tough time, has your faith in God increased over time? Describe what your faith is like currently, today.

As you have learned, and are continuing to learn how to be an Overcomer for Christ, have others in your life noticed anything different about you? If so, what change are they seeing?

Can you use any part of your challenging moments to encourage your friends or family members? Write out a prayer of faith that you would like to see answered when you share your story. God likes the details, so feel free to be specific.

What is the actionable plan for you and God to create an opportunity to share how through Christ you have been an Overcomer? When will you implement this plan?

After your time of sharing, come back and write down how God is, or has answered your prayer.

Write down a few action steps that will allow you to purposefully and intentionally apply this Identity to your life.

I am an Overcomer Screensaver

Chapter Thirteen

I Am Righteous

God made Him who knew no sin to be sin on our behalf, so that in Him we might become the righteousness of God.

2 Corinthians 5:21

It doesn't happen often, but when it does, I like being right. Just ask my wife.

Don't you?

When it happens, it feels oh-so-good.

However, more times than not I get into deeper trouble when I'm trying to be right.

I like making the right statement that others agree with during a meeting. I like making the right decisions about finances, projects, or how much coffee I'm going to drink in the morning. And I like making the right suggestion when choosing a restaurant for date night with my wife. Bonus points are riding on that one.

Can you relate to feeling this way when you know—or think—you're right?

As we traverse through life, an argument can ensue about an opinion of being right. For example, when walking away at the end of a difficult conversation, mentally do you say to yourself, "I was right and they were wrong." Or, do you tend to put a "star" on an imaginary chart showing the wins/losses of arguments in your home.

We live in a world where technology is supposedly helping us make better right decisions about our daily life. "As of August 2023, there *were*

8.93 million apps worldwide… with around 250 million apps downloaded daily."[1] How many apps do you use in a day to help you make the right choice about something? Gaming apps do not count.

Here's a great example of how technology was NOT right. Several years ago, when our family was on vacation, I relied heavily on the little black box attached to the dashboard of my car to get our family safely to our hotel in a city that was quite a distance away from home. We had already driven hundreds of miles and couldn't wait to get checked in and relax in the pristine pool the brochure promised. We were tired and needed a break from being in a small car for countless hours.

As we got closer to the city, we saw all the billboard signs showing attractions every family must stop and visit. Our boys were so excited about all the new things they were seeing, and from the back seat we heard "Can we go there?" "I want to see that!" "Mom and Dad, we gotta eat there," I admit that even my wife and I were getting eager to see some of the colorful attractions shown on each new billboard.

Here's where the problem came in. I put my complete faith and trust in our GPS to make sure we arrived without any problems. We were expecting the device to be accurate with the directions for our vacation.

For most of our trip, everything went well. However, as we began to drive further into the city where our hotel was, we quickly noticed how the GPS was taking us past the tourist part of town. We watched through our bug-stained windows as people walked the candy-, ice cream-, and t-shirt-lined streets. Our GPS said to keep driving straight ahead and like good *robotrons*, we obeyed. We shrugged it off and changed our way of thinking. "Maybe we were mistaken about where the hotel was."

After driving through the town for another few miles, our GPS finally updated its driving information. "Your destination is on the right in half a mile." There was excitement throughout the car. "Make a right turn in a fourth of a mile." We were all looking around at where we were and the excitement turned into worry. The worrying turned to silence. As we made the final "Right turn" into the driveway of what the GPS thought was our destination, we all looked at each other, and then back to where we stopped, and busted out laughing.

Our faithful and trusted GPS, which was supposed to be right, took us to the front gates of the local cemetery.

The GPS was NOT right.

I had put my faith in a small black box that was supposed to improve our vacation experience. I'm not sure it improved our vacation, but it definitely created a great memory we still laugh about today.

I'm almost afraid to turn on the news anymore because each new day there is a group of people declaring, shouting, marching, protesting, and destroying property just because they think they are right. The foundation of what God created is slowly being eroded away just so someone can be right.

It seems everyone has an opinion and everyone thinks they are right. We fight to prove our perspective but fail to listen and understand others. Good thing I never do that (said with just a hint of sarcasm.) We interpret situations based on the way we grew up, the groups we are involved in, the things we have learned, and so on.

Every day, the world shouts, 'I AM RIGHT!' demanding we conform. How can anyone keep up with this ever-changing standard?

Like my faulty GPS, the world claims to guide us to the 'right' destination—but often leads to dead ends. That's why we must turn to God's definition of righteousness, not our own.

RIGHTEOUS

Do you remember back in Chapter 1 – *Blessed*, when I mentioned I struggle with the English language? Here's another great example of how impossible it gets for me. The Merriam-Webster dictionary lists 'right' as an adjective, noun, adverb, and verb—with multiple definitions in each category.

There are actually 33 different ways to use the word 'right,' the first adjective listed is: righteous—'acting in accord with divine or moral law; free from guilt or sin.'[2] Even the dictionary points us toward what Scripture already knows: real righteousness comes from being aligned with God, not proving ourselves right.

I have to give credit to the Merriam-Webster dictionary for providing the perfect segue for the next part of this chapter. Yet, the question remains, how do we become right(eous) and free from guilt and sin?

Paul, the Apostle, was at a crossroads during his third missionary journey as he spent three months in Corinth. Should he travel to the church in Rome, a church he did not establish, or journey on to Jerusalem bringing with him the offering taken up by the Macedonian Christians? Because Paul followed through with delivering the donation, it was there in Jerusalem that he wrote a letter to the believers in Rome which became his *magnum opus*. In Romans 3:10 Paul writes with a heavy hand the following statement, "No one is right with God, no one at all." The New King James Version says it this way, "There is none righteous, no, not one..."

The Jeremiah Study Bible makes a powerful statement regarding to anyone trying to earn a righteous standing. *"These OT words... destroy any hope people might have apart from God. Not even one person can earn a righteous standing in God's eyes. All humanity... is incapable of doing what is right on its own."*[3]

Are we at an impasse here?

The world says everyone, in their own way of thinking, is right. We live in a time where everyone wants to be right, but it's simply impossible. At some point, there has to be a concrete division between what is right and wrong and there needs to be a clear definition of what that means.

As people clamor, fight, and protest to be right about every thought, idea, and statement they can think of, they lose sight of the sinful nature within them. Their idea of being right has become a dynamic contradiction to being righteous in the sight of Christ, our Savior.

Does that mean the arguments, protests, and selfish ways of thinking are all canceled out because as Paul said, '...No one is right...'" or does that add fuel to the fire and make us want to be right even more than before?

A little more than 60 years ago, I was the cutest baby born at the hospital. Well, that's what my mom thought. Babies are cute and cuddly but they are born with a sinful nature into a sinful world. That means the nearly 385,000 babies born globally each day are born with a sinful nature already instilled within them. Just by showing up, these adorable little ones have a strike against them. As Psalm 51:5 states

"Indeed, I was guilty when I was born; I was sinful when my mother conceived me." (HCSB)

That's not a pleasant way to start a life.

Ever since that first breath we took as an infant, we have all been crying out, "I'm right."

I am right because I need to be fed, my diaper needs to be changed, and I need toys to keep me entertained. This right grows ever deeper as we grow older. I am right because I have the best house, car, education, profession, and hybrid dog. I am right because of my societal upbringing, political view, or any one of the new cultural ideologies that are running rampant in our society today.

At some point, we have to get off the "I'm right merry-go-round" and admit, "I'm wrong."

RECONCILIATION

To fully grasp 2 Corinthians 5:21, let's examine the preceding verses (12-20).

It is God's love that compels us – vs. 14

Christ died for all – vs. 15

We should no longer live for ourselves but for Christ – vs. 15

If anyone is in Christ, they are a new creation – vs. 17

Christ's death on the cross equals reconciliation with him – vs. 18

God, through Christ, reconciled the world to Himself – vs. 19

Our sins have been imputed (blotted out never more to be seen) – vs. 19

We are Christ's ambassadors – vs. 20

We have become righteous in Christ – vs. 21

Throughout the history of time, God has always been trying to get our attention. The most significant example was the sacrifice of His only Son, Jesus Christ who died on the cross for our sins. *If* anyone accepts the invitation Christ has offered, their sins are gone forever and they become a new creation in Christ. According to Psalms 103:12, *"As far as the east is from the west, so far has he removed our transgressions from us."*

By acknowledging the fact that our sins have been completely forgiven and removed from us, does that eliminate the need to be right? Please note, that is a question and not a statement. I'm curious to understand the connection between having the whiteboard in heaven that once listed every past, present, and future sin—completely wiped clean once and for all. There will no longer be any evidence of any wrongdoing and the need to be right. As believers in Christ, shouldn't the message be that He is right, that His word is right? Our lives and the decisions we make should absolutely be based on the fact that our Savior is righteous.

So, are we still at an impasse here?

For some, maybe yes. For some, maybe no.

Because of our relationship with Christ, we have automatically been transformed from sinners to righteous saints. In the most humbling way possible, believers can grab ahold of their identity in Christ as I am Righteous. However, those who refuse the relationship offered by Christ are still at the impasse and continue to demand their rights.

In the first section of 2 Corinthians 5:21, we see the impasse turn into the most incredible news we could ever have when it comes to being right.

First, like Paul, we need to accept that *"There is no one righteous, not one?"* However, *"God made Him who knew no sin to be sin on our behalf..."* That's where Christ substituted himself on the cross for our sins.

"God dealt with Christ, not as though He were a sinner, like other men, but as though He were sin itself, absolutely identified with it."[4]

Charles Spurgeon puts it this way

"God has punished Christ instead of me, and therefore he cannot also punish me."[5]

There is not one person on planet Earth that deserves the sacrifice Christ endured. Yet, God became man through Jesus Christ, who became sin on our behalf. Without Christ, there is nothing we can do on our own to become righteous. We can "do" the right things, but that does not make us righteous. Without Christ, we still scream out "I am right" and "I want to be heard".

Within a relationship with Christ, we understand that still, on our own, are not righteous, but it is only Christ, through blotting out our sins, who has made us righteous. That means we are not only heard but loved, comforted, and given a new purpose in life. The screaming can stop and the rejoicing can begin.

The second half of this verse is a celebration.

...so that in him we might become the righteousness of God.

When I met my biological dad for the first time at the age of nineteen, I went to a t-shirt shop at the local mall. I had an idea and I couldn't wait to show it off. I had them make me a t-shirt that said "Proud to be a Miner" on the back of it. After 16-plus years of not knowing anything about my dad, and then meeting him, I wanted to show off the fact that I was proud of my last name. I wanted so badly to become a Miner. I wanted to become like him. I wanted to take on all that came with the last name "Miner."

As believers, we need to understand that "This righteousness is both a legal standing before God and a transformative reality in the believer's life, enabling *us* to live in a way that reflects God's character and holiness."(emphasis added)[6]

With the excitement of meeting my dad, I wanted to reflect on whatever characteristics I inherited from my dad. I wanted to be like him and I wanted to tell the world I belonged to him.

Once I entered into a fully purposeful and intentional relationship with Christ, I now want to be a reflection of God's righteousness.

Becoming *righteous* means we are no longer judged by the world's standards, even though the world may still try to define us by them. We no longer live under the criticism, lies, and corruption the world has to offer.

It's important to note, our sinful behavior does not automatically disappear into thin air. We now have the Holy Spirit living in us, helping us change the condition of our hearts to fall in line with the righteousness that has been bestowed upon us. Now, we are choosing to live right in accordance with God's will and purpose for our lives.

As we continue to grow in Christ, in his righteousness, we reflect more of Christ and less of ourselves. Little by little, changes will begin to happen for us. Those changes will encourage us, and others will begin to notice what the Lord is doing in our lives. This righteous way of living through Christ will begin to bear fruit such as love, joy, peace, patience, kindness, goodness, faithfulness, gentleness, and self-control.

The apostle Paul, who wrote the books of 1 & 2 Corinthians, clearly delineated that because of our Christ-given identity through faith, we can share in the divine righteousness of Christ.

We can say, I am Righteous.

POINTS TO PONDER

Let's go through a quick review of what we just learned.

We are born into a sinful world that demands to be right

Apart from Christ, we will be the ones screaming "I am right" and "Listen to me."

Because not one of us living in a sinful world is righteous, Christ died on our behalf offering to blot out all of our sins, making us righteous in his sight.

Within a relationship with Christ, we can stop the screaming and begin to listen to Christ share with us who we are in Him.

We, through righteous living, actions, and talking, become a reflection of Christ.

True righteousness isn't about proving we're right—it's about surrendering to the One who is right. When we walk in His righteousness, we no longer have to fight for approval—we are already accepted.

An update on the family vacation.

After calling the hotel and speaking to a very nice lady, we received the correct address. She even provided directions from the cemetery to the hotel. The blue-pristine pool was wonderful.

List out some of the messages you constantly hear the world telling you. Screaming at you. Telling you how you should be *right*.

Which one of these messages have you secretly believed? Why?

What does it mean for you knowing God took the form of man through Jesus Christ and died for your sins, blotting them out forever, and making you righteous in His sight?

Write down a few names of friends or family members you think would benefit from knowing this life-saving truth.

Spend time praying for these individuals and asking God to help them become interested in hearing about what He did for them and how it can change their lives. When can you schedule a time to meet with them? Write that down and make a plan to visit with them.

Write down a few action steps that will allow you to purposefully and intentionally apply this Identity to your life.

I am Righteous Screensaver

Chapter Fourteen
I AM SET APART

*Before I formed you in the womb I knew you,
and before you were born; set you apart;
I appointed you...*

Jeremiah 1:5

If I remember correctly, I was in third grade when the teacher asked us to draw something. I don't remember what we were supposed to draw, but I remember putting my head down, focusing on the paper and crayons, and letting my little creative imagination go to work.

Once the art project was done and graded, the teacher handed each student his or her drawing. My anticipation grew because I was proud of what I had drawn and could not wait to take it home and show my mom.

Our teacher smiled as she continued to hand out the artwork to each student. As she walked up and down the rows of desks, more and more students received their drawings; I was still eagerly waiting for her to hand me my drawing.

After the last-colored drawing was placed on whichever student's desk, she stood at the front of the classroom, scanning the room.

I was confused.

Where's my drawing?

Why didn't I get mine back?

I started to feel forgotten—sad and left out.

After my teacher looked over her class of rambunctious students, she called my name, "Jim." Not knowing what to expect I slowly lifted my disappointed head to see what she wanted. "You will notice," she said, "I didn't hand your drawing back to you. Can you please come up to the front and get a hall pass so you can go to the principal's office."

The class erupted in whispers—'Oooo, you're in trouble.' Fear replaced my confusion.

I cautiously stood to my feet and began to walk up to the front of the class. It seemed like it took forever for me to leave my desk and walk that short distance to the front of the room to meet my teacher.

She still had a smile on her face though.

With great trepidation (And no, I don't know any third grader who knows what that word even means!) I reached out to take a hold of the hall pass. Now, with everyone's eyes on me, I had to walk down a different row to the back of the classroom and then out the door.

How could I be in trouble for drawing a picture?

My heart was pounding harder than ever before with each new step I took.

As I opened the door and stepped into the principal's office, the secretary looked up and smiled.

What's with all the smiling, and why am I in trouble?

"Jim, thanks for coming in this morning. Do you know why you are here" she asked.

The obvious answer by the fearful look on my face was, "NO!"

As I approached her desk, she stood to her feet and said, "I'd like to show you something."

Following her hand, she pointed to a special place on the office wall, and there was my drawing.

The office secretary softly told me, "Your teacher said it was the best one out of the whole class and wanted to display it here in the office for everyone to see."

That is a great example of something being set apart for a special purpose.

Years ago, when visiting my mom while she lived out west, we'd go to the small towns filled with artists ranging from glass blowing, painting, and pottery – they were set apart because of their skill set and mastery of a particular medium.

Speaking of pottery, how would you feel if I called you a lump of clay? You know, the cold wet slimy kind that the potter throws onto his potter's wheel, kneading it, molding it, and shaping it into something. Something beautiful and useful.

Most of us would have no idea what to do with a lump of brown slimy clay. However, when the Master Potter is involved, there is creative thought, imagination, and intelligent design carefully integrated into each piece he makes.

Google says the highest price ever paid for a modern or contemporary studio pottery was for a Hans Coper vase, which sold for £381,000, the equivalent of $48,354.81, in 2018.

What?

Imagine this: someone takes clay from the ground, spins it around on a wheel, kneads and molds it, and then carefully transforms it into something *they* think is beautiful. A glaze is brushed on the piece and then into the blazing hot furnace it goes. "The average temperature for a pottery kiln is typically between 2,100°F and 2,300°F." Ouch, that's hot. Then, once the piece is cooled down and removed from the kiln, the potter inspects it, adds a monetary valuation to it, and then places it on a shelf to be sold.

Go ahead and ask the question. "What does a clay pottery piece have to do with the identity of I am Set Apart?" On our own, we are just an ordinary lump of clay just like the person beside us. However, being in the Master's hands, we are being intentionally shaped for a greater purpose.

"BEFORE I FORMED YOU"

Jeremiah 1:5 begins with these four simple words which carry with them a significant meaning. The word *formed* is a keyword here and the meaning is amazing.

to form, fashion, create or to "*to mould into a, form, as a, potter...*"[1]

This Hebrew verb primarily means *that whatever is being created is being done* with intention and purpose. It conveys the idea of a potter shaping clay, highlighting the skill and care involved in the creative process. This term is frequently used to describe God's creative work, emphasizing *His* sovereignty and intentionality in creation. (emphasis added)[2]

Does this sound familiar at all?

Going back to the beginning of scripture, Genesis 2:7 reflects this same connotation when it describes how God made Adam.

Then the LORD God formed a man from the dust of the ground...

The word *formed* from Jeremiah 1:5 has the same definition as the word *formed* used in Genesis 2:7, with both confirming God as the Master Potter. Showcasing these two examples defines God as consistent in what he does.

It all comes down to the reality of what Isaiah wrote so long ago,

"Yet you, LORD, are our Father. We are the clay, you are the potter; we are all the work of your hand." Isaiah 64:8

"I KNEW YOU"

God told Jeremiah that before he was even conceived in the womb he was already known. Before the clay was found to form Jeremiah, God sat down at his heavenly desk and began to write down every detail about Jeremiah (this is how I would imagine God designing his creations). What he would look like, which country, culture, and people group he would be born into. Every detail about Jeremiah was so important that God wrote it down in a book, hence, God sat down at a heavenly desk.

"Your eyes saw my unformed body; all the days ordained for me were written in your book before one of them came to be." Psalm 139:16

As the Master Potter was forming each one of us he already knew the exact date and time we were to be conceived and then born. He knew of our position in life along with the difficult and celebratory events that would occur in our lives.

The Hebrew word for "*I knew you*" ( )□□□□□is (yah-DAH, pronounced yah-dah) and in the biblical context it often implies a *deep, personal, and relational knowledge,* such as the *intimate relationship between* God and His people... (emphasis added)[3]

This *knowing* goes far deeper than a general acquaintance-type friendship. This yah-DAH, *knowing*, is profoundly relational and experiential including an emotional and spiritual understanding of someone.

Unlike the drawing I created in third grade, God knew what he wanted to form first. There was an intentional knowing before the forming.

As a parent of two incredible sons, I'd like to think I "know" them pretty well. It's easy to see their separate personalities, attitudes, and opinions about life. Yet, the knowing I have with my two sons is completely different from that of our Creator.

Can we all agree that God knows his children better than earthly parents know theirs?

Psalms 144:3 and 4 pose a great question.

"LORD, what are human beings that you care for them, mere mortals that you think of them? They are like a breath; their days are like a fleeting shadow."

It says we are "...mere mortals..." a "...breath," or "...fleeting shadow". This description becomes the true indicator of who we are in comparison to God. We are very little and he is really, really, big. However, even though that may be true, we are still something made by the hands of the Master Potter. He has purposely set us apart for "good works" to advance his kingdom, to be a reflection of his Son, Jesus Christ. In this next section we will learn specific ways believers have been set apart for God's glory.

"I SET YOU APART"

I did not have any knowledge my third-grade picture would end up in the principal's office. Picking up a crayon or colored pencil, I simply drew—but It was my teacher who decided to set my picture apart from all the others in my class.

These four simple words, *"...I set you apart..."* refer to the fact that God did not want Jeremiah to be like everyone else. His clay masterpiece had a greater purpose than to sit on a shelf to collect dust. This vessel was to be set apart, consecrated, and holy. The Hebrew definition here means

"...designated for divine service or worship."[4]

Here are several reasons why believers are set apart...
To be a reflection of Christ
To declare praises
To be set free from sin
To fulfill a purpose
To be anointed and equipped

Keep in mind, being set apart does not mean you're isolated—it means you've been chosen, shaped, and called for something greater.

"I APPOINTED YOU"

Here is the crux of why Jeremiah was formed and set apart, this consecrated servant was appointed a prophet to the nations.

The forty years of ministry for this young prophet started with a conversation that loosely went like this,

God: "Jeremiah, I knew you before you were formed. I set you apart making you holy for such a time as this and now I am appointing you as a prophet to the nations."

Jeremiah: "Hey, can we talk about this? I'm young and afraid of what everyone will say about me."

God: "Yes, I know these things, but... my calling has already been placed on you."

Jeremiah was about 17 years old when God put this heavy and demanding appointment upon him. He became a prophet to the tribes of Benjamin and Judah even though he was timid and reluctant to accept the calling. Because of his age, Jeremiah was fearful of what others would think and say about him.

While walking to the front of my third-grade classroom to take the hall pass, all I could hear were the comments from the other students. That led to the confusion and frustration of not knowing why I was being sent to the principal's office. Listening to the other kids drown out the real reason my teacher had a soft and gentle smile on her face. She knew the real reason behind the hall pass.

Just like Jeremiah, we often wrestle with self-doubt when God calls us. But fear and distractions should not keep us from stepping into our purpose.

Some might think since Jeremiah was an Old Testament prophet who lived thousands of years ago, this does not apply to our current life or situation.

That is a great thought.

However, the first eight verses of Jeremiah represent a consistent message throughout scripture.

God creates and forms man for the sole purpose of having a relationship with them. Man disobeys God, bringing sin into the world. God loves his creation so much that he appoints men and women to call nations back to their original purpose with the eventual birth, death, and resurrection of our creator's only Son, Jesus Christ.

It's easy to fall back on the thought, "Look how God set Jeremiah apart, but that's the Old Testament and I'm not sure I feel set apart for anything right now." Therefore, let's consider your appointment may not be to speak to nations like Jeremiah, but it may be to teach a child, encourage a neighbor, lead a team, or serve faithfully in the background. Whatever the calling, it's been set apart for you.

From the beginning of time with Adam and Eve in the Garden of Eden, until this very moment, God has been constantly pursuing the very thing he created, us, you and me.

Approximately 2,000 years ago, after Christ was raised from the dead, he appeared to the twelve disciples and presented them with The Great Commission. I am sure there were a variety of other reasons why Christ chose each one of the disciples, but in the end, they were chosen to write books of the Bible, start churches, and they become missionaries who would spread the good news about Jesus Christ.

It seemed like the longest moment a third-grade student could ever experience, but I did it. I stood in the principal's office, taking in the moment as I looked at my drawing. Now I understood why my teacher kept smiling. I understood why the secretary was smiling and now I was smiling.

I couldn't wait for my mom to get home from work so I could tell her this great news. I wanted to see her smile as well.

Some of us reading this chapter have experienced tough setbacks in life and instead of experiencing the joy of being set apart, you have felt more like you have been pushed down and disregarded. You have tried to keep your head above water even though the waves keep coming from every direction, crashing over you. Your hope dwindles as the tides of life sweep over you again and again.

When the pain and disappointments of life feel overwhelming, you may reach a breaking point—one where surrender seems like the only option. The taunts of 'He's in trouble' from childhood can become louder than the truth: that your Creator has known, formed, set apart, and appointed you for a purpose.

So, why even try anymore?

In the book of Psalms, David was deeply transparent when it came to being completely honest with God. Chapters and verses declare the praises of God while in others, David questions if God is still present in his life. There is a constant ebb and flow that oftentimes comes back to a humble servant falling to his knees with whispers of gratitude. The whole chapter of Psalms 139 is a great example of what this looks like.

"For you created my inmost being; you knit me together in my mother's womb."

Instead of throwing up our hands in defeat we now, through a relationship with our creator can raise our hand in praise to the one who formed, knew, set us apart, and appointed us. Even before the world was created, God had a purpose for each one of us. Before the six days of creation, God had already set us apart to be holy.

POINTS TO PONDER

You are not an accident. You are not forgotten. Before time began, God formed you, knew you, set you apart, and appointed you. Now, He is calling you to walk in that identity. Will you answer?

Scripture consistently provides examples of how the Master Potter formed you before time even existed. Regardless of past or current events in your life, write down your reflections on what it means to have all the details of your life written down in God's book.

Do you think there was a glitch in the system when God wrote your story? Describe the glitch.

This identity, I am Set Apart, explains we are more than just a bunch of cells that have been randomly collected through space and brought together. There's a defined purpose for you being right where you are at this time in your life. How do you believe God has set you apart for such a time as this?

Being Set Apart means you are willing to accept the appointment you have been given. Write down a few action steps that will allow you to purposefully and intentionally apply this Identity to your life.

I am Set Apart Screensaver

Chapter Fifteen

I Am Valuable

*For God so loved the world
that he gave his one and only Son,
that whoever believes in him
shall not perish but have eternal life.*

John 3:16

Would you agree that everything in our world has a price tag on it?

I propose that everything and everyone has been labeled with some amount of valuation from the beginning of time.

Whether it's monetary value or someone's opinion, this valuing process has become second nature for many of us. Here are some thoughts that might run through our minds as we enter a store. While looking around, we begin the game of "Whoa, I like that, but it's definitely not worth that price." Or, "That item is way too expensive, but if my friends see me with it, then they will like me even more." The subconscious thought would be, "I will be valued."

We see some type of valuation everywhere we look. There are colorful rectangular stickers and white tags that hang attached to a tiny string on the prettiest dresses. Large cardboard tags with the branding logo hanging from a sleeve or stapled on a pocket. Restaurants show the value of a meal with either a fancy chalk-filled menu board or a laminated tri-fold menu. Let's not forget about the car lot filled with new and shiny cars and trucks showing all the features in small print and the valuation in large print at the bottom of the sticker.

TOP TEN

Growing up, I always found it fascinating to hear about the top ten millionaires who made it onto some national list. By today's standards, we no longer give millionaires a second thought because the list has changed by a few zeros to billionaires.

Every year Forbes magazine collects data that culminates with a list of the richest people in the world. For 2024 the article is titled World's Billionaires List and here are the numbers that might make you sit back and just say, "Hmmm."

The United States comes in first boasting a record 813 billionaires worth a combined $5.7 trillion.

China is second with 473 billionaires worth $1.7 trillion

India ranks third with 200 billionaires worth $300 billion in wealth.

Currently, the richest man in the world has an empire worth a staggering $233 billion valuation.[1]

Let's continue down this fantasy road of adding value to things and learn about one of the most expensive toys in the world: the History Supreme Yacht worth a whopping 4.8 billion dollars. Here are a couple of the features this yacht is decorated with.

It is coated in solid gold and platinum – over 220,462 pounds of precious metals.

The master bedroom is decorated with meteorite stone accents and a genuine tyrannosaurus Rex Bone.[2]

I live on a farm with ten chickens, four cats, and a high-spirited puppy. How am I supposed to understand having a bedroom with meteorite accents and a T-rex bone in it?

Guinness World Records says the International Space Station is the most expensive thing ever created, costing $150 billion to design and build.[3]

As I just mentioned, my wife and I are blessed and happy with a nice farmhouse on a few acres with some chickens, and cats. My wife would like a couple of goats, b-uuu-ttt (no pun intended) we will have to see about that. I value getting four eggs from our four chickens every day. Some days are good with the girls sitting on their nests and laying beautiful colored eggs, while other days they fall short.

I must admit that seeing the staggering list above is impressive, to say the least. However, they are so impressive and yet impossible for me to fully comprehend. In other words, I will never have a complete concept of what millions or billions of dollars look like, and I am completely fine with that.

For those of us who do not have a 7, 10, or 13-figure bank account, we may tend to put a value on the square footage of our homes, or how many homes we have. What about having the newest car or truck? The diamond ring on the left finger always gets attention, right? Or, for some of you, it's how many pairs of sneakers or high-heels you have hidden away in your closet. Let's get a little personal and ask about the 401k or pension statement.

All of the items listed above are examples of things we add value to. Whether it is monetary or societal, at the end of the day, we still place a value on something or someone.

Items that are meant to be sold require a price tag to demonstrate their worth to a buyer—I understand that. However, the problem arises when we, as believers, begin to internalize that concept, equating money, power, and prestige with our self-worth. On that point, I adamantly disagree. Our value is not determined by the wealth or possessions we accumulate over time. Job positions, social status, and even where we live are simply circumstances, not measures of our worth. The sense of importance we attach to them is fleeting, a false security that will one day fade away.

"Do not store up for yourselves treasures on earth, where moths and vermin destroy, and where thieves break in and steal." Matthew 6:19

Let's go down a rabbit hole together for a moment and ask this question, "What if the value we desire from these things and people is an outward expression of an internal longing to *be* valued yourself?"

Again, just a thought that will be answered later on.

Let's ask another question, "Why throw all those valuations your way?"

Well, simply put, that is the world we live in. I'm not going to expound on researching when people become so focused on gaining self worth from something.

Wait...

Wait, just a second.

I don't have to because I already know when the values of people changed. It was that moment in time when one single disastrous decision changed the world forever. It was the exact moment when both Adam and Eve sinned while in the Garden of Eden.

EQUALITY WITH GOD

Adam was created in the image of God while a single rib from him became the foundation for Eve being created. This relationship was the most perfect union between God, man, and woman, and has never been fully experienced since.

Their whole life was complete and established on a relationship with the Creator, Himself.

"God would walk in the Garden of Eden in the cool of the day to fellowship with Adam and Eve." Genesis 1:3

During this intimate time of fellowship with their Creator, Adam and Eve were complete because they were made in the image of God. They were entirely and wholly valued. God had such a high esteem for them that when placing them in the Garden he gave them the responsibility of being caretakers of everything he had created. They could see the beauty in each other and everything that had been created around them. However, those things did not give them value. The value they experienced was solely based upon who they were within fellowship with God.

Adam and Eve were granted three very special privileges within this relationship.

First, we read in Genesis 1:3 that they were in communion with God; they walked and talked with Him every day. Currently, the only way we can communicate with God is through prayer and worship.

There has to be some level of curiosity as to what it was like for Adam and Eve to walk in the Garden completely shameless fellowshipping with their creator. Our understanding of perfection can't begin to describe what this must have been like—because God is the very definition of perfection.

Secondly, they knew God as He *was*. Their minds were not clouded by falsehoods or half-truths. There was never a thought about their value coming from something they accumulated. There were no pretensions or self-opinionated guesses about the other person. Their thoughts towards God and each other were pure, as was God's towards them.

I must admit there are times when going before God in prayer I have my own agenda which is based on expectations I've learned throughout my life. Adam and Eve had something that will never be experienced this side of heaven again. There was a promised relationship based on the true *value* God had given to them and I can't wait to experience that when I get to heaven.

"Lastly, they possessed spiritual life. They were alive not just physically, but in every sense of the word their souls were alive."[4]

Can we even ask what "...their souls were alive" means?

Absolutely, and we should.

Adam and Eve were more than just physically alive, their souls were brought to life and sustained through the compassionate and divine nature of who God was and now is. God walked in the garden with them, calling to them so they would hear his voice and come running. There was a place in their hearts that only God could fill. There is a place in our hearts that God can only fill.

A few years after his death in 1662, Blaise Pascal, a 17th-century philosopher and mathematician, wrote *Pensées (Thoughts), a collection of fragments in defense of Christianity*. He writes the following that supports the idea there is a special place in our hearts that only God can fill.

> What is it then that this desire and this inability proclaim to us, but that there was once in man a true happiness of which there now remain to him only the mark and empty trace, which he in vain tries to fill from all his surroundings, seeking from things absent the help he does not obtain in things

present? But these are all inadequate, because the infinite abyss can only be filled by an infinite and immutable object, that is to say, only by God Himself.[5]

Search, as we might, nothing in this world will ever compare to the deep and immense, holy and caring, saving and gracious relationship we can have with our Heavenly Father.

THEN

Then it happened.

Satan found a soft spot within God's creation, something he understood but Adam and Eve did not. The trick was to get them to be curious enough to want the low-hanging fruit. The message was "Taste and see" then you will be an equal with God and have just as much knowledge as he has right now. Do this one thing and you will be the same as the one who created you. That's the lie that has been passed down for thousands of years which corrupted the relationship Eve had with her creator.

"...and you will be like God, knowing good and evil." Genesis 3:5

Eve may have started down this disastrous road but Adam was no different.

It's possible the expectation he had in disobeying God was that Eve would value him for stepping up and being a "man" because he did what she wanted. He may have also thought that if he ate this fruit, he would be equal to God and smarter than Eve.

Maybe.

Regardless of the actual conversation between Adam, Eve, and the snake, being equal to God and having the same knowledge had a value placed on it.

This was the beginning of putting price tags or a value on something or someone other than God, and we have continued doing so ever since.

THE OLD WAY

When sin entered the world, it shattered the perfect relationship between God and humanity. But God, unwilling to abandon the ones He loved, set in motion a plan to bring us back to Him.

The Jeremiah Study Bible provides the following information on how this holy relationship would be implemented.

"The Lord... raised up Israel as a distinct people group; the descendants of Abraham and Sarah were to be the means whereby He would draw other people to His holy worship. For this to work, the Hebrew people had to be holy – they were to be set apart *for the Lord* as a light to the Gentiles, a repository of the knowledge of God."[6]

But, how do you make an unholy people holy?

This is where the book of Leviticus comes in.

The first few chapters of this historical Old Testament book help us understand what the Israelites put into place. At the time there were five different types of Sacrifices or Offerings, three different Special Sacrificial Practices, the Role of the Priesthood followed by Regulations and Procedures. Each of these rituals was practiced up until the day Jesus was crucified.

Old Testament sacrifices and offerings were seen as a representation to atone for the sins of man, but they were never a perfect solution. They were only temporary.

These sacrificial offerings were good but God began to prepare the world for something that would last forever, redemption through his Son, Jesus Christ.

THE NEW WAY

There are more than 300 Old Testament prophecies that occurred over the span of 1,000 years concerning the Birth, Ministry, Suffering, Death, and Resurrection of Jesus Christ.

Even before time began, God deeply desired fellowship with mankind. I would go so far as to say there was an aching or longing in his heart to be in a relationship with his ultimate creation.

"God is faithful, who has called you into fellowship with his Son, Jesus Christ our Lord." 1 Corinthians 1:9

God has been trying to get our attention ever since the relationship was severed by the one who "...kills, steals, and destroys." Since the fall of mankind, we have been separated from God because of our sinful nature.

God's yearning for fellowship with us was so great that he took it upon himself to reestablish the relationship with his creation. God designed a perfect plan, an eternal plan that superseded all of the Old Testament sacrifices and offerings. This plan was to send His only Son, Jesus Christ in the form of a man, to become the ultimate end-all sacrifice for everyone.

As mentioned before, prophecies foretold of the birth of a baby boy that would be called Immanuel.

"...and they shall call His name Immanuel, which is translated, "God with us."" Matthew 1:23

Wait a minute.

Did you catch that or did it almost slip by?

This baby, Jesus Christ, would be called Immanuel, meaning "God with us."

This is a full-circle moment for me and I hope it is for you as well.

God had a way for us to come back into a full relationship with him through the birth of a baby. This was no ordinary baby though. This baby was the full embodiment of God himself and, just like in the Garden of Eden, God once again came down to mankind to fellowship with us.

But, why?

Why has God continually been trying to reconnect with a sinful people? Most of us would have given up on each other thousands of years ago, leaving each to their own demise.

It all comes down to the first six words of this verse we are studying.

"For God so loved the world..."

God, Elohiym, Yahweh, in all of his majesty and power, loved the inhabitants of the world with an agapaó (agape) or unconditional love. This type of love and traverse the centuries of time, calling men and women, boys and girls, into fellowship with him.

Absolutely not!

This type of love was Yahweh understanding his creation. You and I were lost and steeped in sin that separated us from God and he saw how his creation was choosing to be separated from him and he was displeased. Can I say that he was displeased and disheartened?

The 59th Chapter of Isaiah describes our sinful nature. It's a great illustration of what God is dealing with while trying to love his valued creation.

"But your iniquities have separated you from your God; your sins have hidden his face from you, so that he will not hear." Isaiah 59:2

However, because God still loved us but hated the sin we choose to live in every day, Jesus Christ became the lamb, taking our place on the sacrificial altar mentioned so many times in the Old Testament.

Think about it for a moment. Jesus knew that at some point in time, his Father would look over at him and say "It's time." There was already a foreknowledge on Christ's behalf that he would come to earth as a baby and sacrifice his life for ours because of sin.

Christ died a horrible and gruesome death on the cross for our sins. He substituted his life for ours. He took on every imaginable and unimaginable sin Satan could ever devise, willingly suffering for his creation.

But Jesus' death was not the end of the story. On the third day after his crucifixion, Jesus conquered death and rose again as King of Kings and Lord of Lords. All because he valued you and me so much!

Never, has there been someone in the history of the world who cared about people so much that he would lay down his life for the sole purpose of forgiveness and eternal relationship.

Once all the riches, toys, houses, jewelry, vehicles, and fluffy hybrid pets fade away, what are we left with? What will we have? In the end? It will be just ourselves, standing before God, one on one.

I'm not sure how to fully describe the feeling of knowing that God values me. Of course, I am deeply grateful—but even "thankful" seems inadequate compared to what God has done. Understanding the profound difference between merely being created in God's image and actively being in a relationship with Him is far more significant than any billionaire ranking Forbes magazine could print. God took the first step toward us by sending His Son, offering us the free gift of salvation. Now, the choice is ours—what will we do with that gift?

Just as Adam and Eve were given the ability to choose—either to live in full relationship with their Creator or to believe a lie and disobey—so too are we faced with a similar decision. Will we choose eternal life with Christ, or will we follow the world's constant message of self-sufficiency and personal "rightness," ultimately leading to separation from Him?

You see, God created the perfect relationship with mankind and He valued Adam and Eve so much. From that instantaneous moment when they disobeyed, they broke that valued relationship off for the rest of us. We would never be able to experience the same valued relationship with God as they did.

From the very beginning of time, God gave us free will to do whatever we wanted. In the end, though, it all comes down to the most important decision you will ever make in your life. The one decision to ask Christ to forgive you of your sins and come into your life so you can live for him because you are Valuable.

You see, the Word of God is very clear on the consequences of this broken relationship.

Living a life that rejects God is willingly and knowingly separating yourself from the one who created you. The one that values you the most. This disconnected relationship removes you from any of the prior identities written in this devotional study guide. They do not belong to you. Continuing in a life of sin trying to be equal with and having more knowledge than God will only bring death upon you that will last for all eternity.

In John 14:6, Jesus states the following,

"I am the way and the truth and the life. No one comes to the Father except through me."

Yet, God demonstrated how much he loved and valued us by sending his only Son to die on the cross for you and me. This free gift will take us through eternity with the one who has given us so much value.

For God so loved the world
that he gave his one and only Son,

that whoever believes in him
shall not perish but have eternal life.

Here's what scripture says about the separation and saving decision you can make right now.

ROMANS ROAD

Romans 3:23 says, "For all have sinned and fall short of the glory of God."

Romans 6:23 says, "For the wages of sin is death, but the gift of God is eternal life in Christ Jesus our Lord."

Romans 5:8 says, "But God demonstrates his own love for us in this: While we were still sinners, Christ died for us."

Romans 10:9, 10 says, "If you declare with your mouth, "Jesus is Lord," and believe in your heart that God raised him from the dead, you will be saved."

PRAYER

At this time, if you would like to change the direction of your life then here's a simple prayer for you.

Lord, I come before you as a sinner and I ask for your forgiveness. I believe you died and rose from the dead and I choose to turn away from my sinful life. I invite you into my heart to rule and reign. I place my trust in you and choose to follow you as my Lord and Savior. Amen.

CONGRATULATIONS!

If you prayed this prayer, congratulations, and welcome to the family of God. You have now been adopted into a family of brothers and sisters who want to love and encourage you. Today, you can stand forgiven and loved.

One of the most important things you can do right now is to find a good church that preaches what the Bible says, and not what today's culture is screaming at you. Also, tell others about your life-changing decision. As a matter of fact, I'd love to be one of the first people you tell.

Feel free to contact me through my website: www.rebrandednchrist.com and tell me about your decision. I'd love to welcome and encourage you as you begin your new journey as a Forgiven Child of God.

If you've walked this journey of identity with me, I hope you see now that your value is unshakable—not because of what you've done, but because of what Christ has done for you. You are not defined by the world's price tags or rankings. You are defined by the cross. And that makes you priceless.

POINTS TO PONDER

Let's not forget about those of you who have already accepted Christ as your Savior. In that regard, I hope this devotional study guide has been an encouragement as you walked through each one of the identities presented.

Your value isn't found in wealth, possessions, or status. It's found in Christ alone. And when trials come, you can stand firm—because your worth is unshakable in Him. You can withstand the chaos that swirls around you because of the identities in Christ you have learned about.

If today is the day you prayed the "sinners prayer", write down the date, time, and where you were at. Use this as a reminder for down the road.

If you have accepted Christ at some other time in your life, write down that date, time, and place so you can always come back to it as well.

Find a Bible-believing church in your area that will help you grow in the Lord. When can you start attending this church?

Write down the names of three people you can talk to about the decision you made to follow Christ. Again, you can count me in as the first one.

For those who have already been walking with the Lord, write down at least three ways you are committed to sharing God's Valuable story with others.

Lastly, we all know of someone who could benefit from being valued. Someone who needs to be set free from the wages of sin and death. Write their names down and begin to pray for them. You will be amazed at what God can do through your prayers.

Write down a few action steps that will allow you to purposefully and intentionally apply this Identity to your life.

I am Valuable Screensaver

AFTERWORD

Are you looking for a place where you can be real, be heard, and be encouraged in your walk with Christ?

If so, I want to personally invite you to check out The Redeemed, a men's ministry that has made a lasting impact on my life since I connected with them in September 2022.

Men face real struggles every day—battles with purpose, identity, relationships, and faith.

The goal of The Redeemed is to provide men with a supportive, communal environment where they can discuss their problems, worries, and feelings of "brokenness" without fear of being judged or censored. And while the values of The Redeemed are rooted in the redemption God has granted us—even before we've even asked for it, we welcome men of any faith or no faith at all. We present God's redemption not as a trophy that can be won only by the worthy, but as a path that is open to all.[1]

Scan the QR code below and check out the website and see if this is the community you've been looking for. Who knows? Maybe I'll see you in an online group soon!

www.theredeemed.com

ABOUT THE AUTHOR

Jim and his beloved wife, Cristee', of 27 years call the picturesque rolling hills of Northeast Iowa home. Even though they are empty-nesters, with their two sons and incredible daughter-in-law living nearby, Jim and his wife live on a small family farm with ten spirited chickens, four affectionate cats, and one very rambunctious puppy.

Jim is a member of The Forge Men's Ministry Leadership Team at his local church, where they focus on inwardly discipling men so they can move outward as a reflection of Christ. His passion for mentoring men extends beyond local borders, touching lives nationally as an online group leader with The Redeemed Men's Ministry, an organization dedicated to supporting men through their faith journey. Jim actively mentors men at the local, national, and international levels, equipping them to grow in their faith and relationship with Christ.

Beyond his ministry work, Jim enjoys spending time with his family and tending to the daily rhythms of life on the farm.

ENDNOTES

Introduction

1. 2020. "PMC PubMed Central." *National Library of Medicine.* July 1. Accessed March 22, 2025. https://pmc.ncbi.nlm.nih.gov/articles/PMC7329252/.

I am Blessed

1. https://biblehub.com/greek/2128.htm

2. n.d. *Merriam-Webster.* Accessed April 1, 2025. https://www.merriam-webster.com/dictionary/eulogy.

3. Mark 14:61; Luke 1:68; Romans 1:25, 9:5; 2 Corinthians 1:3, 11:31; Ephesians 1:3, and 1 Peter 1:3

4. n.d. *Merriam-Webster.* Accessed April 1, 2025. https://www.merriam-webster.com/dictionary/eulogy.

5. https://biblehub.com/greek/2127.htm

6. https://biblehub.com/greek/2129.htm

7. n.d. *Bible Hub.* Accessed 2024. https://biblehub.com/greek/2129.htm.

I am Chosen

1. Luke 5:8

2. n.d. *Bible Hub.* Accessed 2024. https://biblehub.com/greek/1588.htm.

3. n.d. *Bible Hub*. Accessed 2024. https://biblehub.com/greek/1588.htm.

4. https://biblehub.com/greek/2406.htm

5. https://biblehub.com/greek/strongs_40.htm
   https://biblehub.com/greek/strongs_1484.htm

6. https://biblehub.com/greek/4047.htm

7. https://biblehub.com/greek/703.htm

I am Complete

1. https://biblehub.com/greek/4137.htm

2. 2 Corinthians 10:5

I am Confident

1. n.d. *Merriam-Webster Dictionary*. Accessed March 25, 2025, 2025. https://www.merriam-webster.com/dictionary/confident#synonyms.

2. n.d. *BibleHub.com*. Accessed 2024. https://biblehub.com/greek/3982.htm.

3. n.d. *BibleHub.com*. Accessed 2024. https://biblehub.com/greek/4102.htm.

4. n.d. *BibleHub.com*. Accessed 2024. https://biblehub.com/greek/4102.htm.

5. n.d. "courageous.cassie." *Instagram*. Accessed 2024. https://www.instagram.com/courageous.cassie/reel/DHbQNgyOIkW/if-god-placed-a-goliath-in-front-of-you-its-because-he-knows-theres-a-david-insi/.

6. 2025. "How Many Ads Do We See a Day?" *siteefy*. January 13. Accessed March 25, 2025. https://siteefy.com/how-many-ads-do-we-see-a-day.

I am a Conqueror

1. n.d. *Bible Hub*. Accessed 2024. https://biblehub.com/romans/8-37.htm.

2. n.d. *Bible Hub*. Accessed 2024. https://biblehub.com/greek/5245.htm.

3. n.d. *Bible Hub*. Accessed 2024. https://biblehub.com/greek/5228.htm.

4. n.d. *Bible Hub*. Accessed 2024. https://biblehub.com/greek/3528.htm.

5. n.d. *Bible Hub*. Accessed 2024. https://biblehub.com/greek/3529.htm.

6. 2017. *PodBean*. November 8. Accessed 2024. https://natelarkin.podbean.com/.

7. The Jeremiah Study Bible, NKJV, Worthy Publishing, Nashvillle, TN, Romans 8:37 footnotes, page1556

8. The Jeremy Study Bible, NKJV, Worthy Publishing, Nashville, TN, Romans 8:34, footnotes, page 1556

I Can Do All Things

1. n.d. "successaddictives." *Instagram*. Accessed February 12, 2025. https://www.instagram.com/successaddictives/p/DEht_INCWXW/?img_index=5.

2. Cole, Paul Louis. n.d. "christianmensnetwork." *Instagram.* Accessed February 12, 2025. https://www.instagram.com/christianmensnetwork/p/DDSAlFOv1gT/?locale=es&hl=bg.

3. n.d. *Bible Hub.* Accessed 2024. https://biblehub.com/philippians/4-13.htm#commentary.

4. n.d. *Bible Hub.* Accessed April 1, 2025. https://biblehub.com/greek/1743.htm.

5. laurenzoeller. n.d. *Instagram.* Accessed February 12, 2025. https://www.instagram.com/p/DA0hOI8SNrF/.

I am Fearless

1. n.d. *BibleHub.* Accessed February 12, 2025. https://biblehub.com/greek/1167.htm.

2. Tom and Sharon Rich, Gerry and Tracy Mitts, Tom and Darla Butikofer, Lee and Diane Boleyn, interview by Jim Miner. 2024.

3. n.d. *Bible Hub.* Accessed 2024. https://biblehub.com/greek/1411.htm.

4. Ephesians 1:19-20

5. 1 John 4:18

6. n.d. *Bible Hub.* Accessed 2024. https://biblehub.com/greek/4998.htm.

I Am Forgiven

1. n.d. *BibleHub.* Accessed March 12, 2025. https://biblehub.com/greek/629.htm%20March%2012.

2. n.d. *Merriam-Webster Dictionar.* Accessed March 11, 2025. https://www.merriam-webster.com/dictionary/redeem#dictionary-entry-1.

3. Bennett, Josh McDowell and Ben. 2021. *Free to Thrive.* Nashville, TN: Josh McDowell Ministry.

4. Luke 23:34

5. Staff, Mayo Clinic. 2022. "Healthy Lifestyle." *Mayo Clinic.* November 22. Accessed March 18, 2025. https://www.mayoclinic.org/healthy-lifestyle/adult-health/in-depth/forgiveness/art-20047692?p=1.

6. Staff, Reviewed by Psychology Today. n.d. "Psychology Today - Forgiveness." *www.psychologytoday.com.* Accessed 2024. https://www.psychologytoday.com/us/basics/forgiveness.

7. Chip Dodd, Ph.D. 2014. *The Voice of the Heart.* Chris Dodd Resources. pages 126 & 128

8. Chip Dodd, Ph.D. 2014. *The Voice of the Heart.* Chris Dodd Resources. page 128

I am God's Child

1. n.d. *Bible Hub.* Accessed 2024. https://biblehub.com/john/1-12.htm#commentary.

2. 2 Corinthians 5:17

3. Galatians 2:20

4. Ephesians 1:4-5

5. Anderson, Neil T. 2020. *Victory Over the Darkness.* Bloomington, MN: Bethany House, page 33

6. Bennett, Josh McDowell and Ben. 2021. *Free to Thrive: How Your Hurt, Struggles, and Deepest Longings Can Lead to a Fulfilling Life.* Nashville: Thomas Nelson, page 12

7. n.d. *Bible Hub.* Accessed 2024. https://biblehub.com/greek/5043.htm.

I am God's Friend

1. https://www.merriam-webster.com/dictionary/friend#h1

2. n.d. *Bible Hub.* Accessed 2024. https://biblehub.com/greek/1401.htm.

3. Galatians 3:26-29

4. n.d. *Bible Hub.* Accessed 2024. https://biblehub.com/greek/5384.htm.

5. n.d. *Collins.* Accessed April 1, 2025. https://www.collinsdictionary.com/us/dictionary/english/confidant.

6. n.d. *Bible Hub.* Accessed April 1, 2025. https://biblehub.com/john/15-15.htm#study.

I am Made by God

1. n.d. *Bible Hub.* Accessed 2024. https://biblehub.com/greek/4161.htm.

2. Keller, Dr. Timothy. n.d. "Vocation - Discerning Your Calling (Tim Keller)." *SCRIBD.* Accessed 2025. https://www.scribd.com/document/148804395/Vocation-Discerning-Your-Calling-Tim-Keller.

3. 2025. "Believers Are God's Masterpiece, His Poiema." *Precept Austin.* February 10. Accessed February 12, 2025. https://www.preceptaustin.org/gods_masterpiece-poiema_greek_word_study.

4. 1989. "MP3: When the Night is Falling FL." *Dennis Jernigan.* November 7-8. Accessed 2025. https://dennisjernigan.com/store/product.php?c=24&p=3912.

5. n.d. *Bible Hub*. Accessed 2025. https://biblehub.com/jeremiah/29-11.htm.

I am an Overcomer

1. n.d. *Bible Hub*. Accessed 2025. https://biblehub.com/greek/4100.htm.

I am Righteous

1. 2023. *RipenApps*. August 16. Accessed March 10, 2025. https://ripenapps.com/blog/mobile-app-industry-statistics/.

2. n.d. *Merriam-Webster Dictionary*. Accessed 2025. https://www.merriam-webster.com/dictionary/right.

3. Jeremiah Study Bible (Nashville: Thomas Nelson, 2013), 1547

4. n.d. *BibleHub*. Accessed 2024. https://biblehub.com/commentaries/ellicott/2_corinthians/5.htm.

5. n.d. "spurgeonbooks." *Instagram*. Accessed 2025. https://www.instagram.com/spurgeonbooks/p/DA3Px2PSgsd/?img_index=1.

6. n.d. *BibleHub*. Accessed 2024. https://biblehub.com/2_corinthians/5-21.htm#study.

I am Set Apart

1. n.d. *Bible Hub*. Accessed 2024. https://biblehub.com/hebrew/3335.htm.

2. n.d. *Bible Hub*. Accessed 2025. https://biblehub.com/hebrew/3335.htm.

3. n.d. *Bible Hub*. Accessed 2025. https://biblehub.com/hebrew/strongs_3045.htm.

4. n.d. *Bible Hub*. Accessed 2025. https://biblehub.com/hebrew/6942.htm.

I am Valuable

1. 2024. "Forbes World's Billionaires List: The Richest in 2024." *Forbes*. Accessed 2025. https://www.forbes.com/billionaires/.

2. 2024. "15 of the Most Expensive Things in the World in 2024." *Yahoo! fiance*. June 2024. Accessed January 2025. https://finance.yahoo.com/news/15-most-expensive-things-world-201004398.html?guccounter=1.

3. n.d. "Most Expensive Man-Made Object." *Guiness World Records*. Accessed 2025. https://www.guinnessworldrecords.com/world-records/most-expensive-man-made-object.

4. 2013. "fyi Before and After the Fall." In *The Jeremiah Study Bible*, 9. Worthy Publishing, page 9

5. n.d. *Project Gutenberg*. Accessed 14 2025, 2025. https://gutenberg.org/cache/epub/18269/pg18269-images.html.

6. 2013. "Leviticus, Book Introduction." In *The Jeremiah Study Bible*, 129. Worthy Publishing.

Afterword

1. https://theredeemed.com/about/

www.ingramcontent.com/pod-product-compliance
Lightning Source LLC
Chambersburg PA
CBHW030453100526
44580CB00009B/117/J